FOLLOW THE
SCIENCE TO
SCHOOL

Evidence-based Practices
for Elementary Education

Edited by

MICHAEL J. PETRILLI,
BARBARA DAVIDSON
and **KATHLEEN CARROLL**

First Published 2022

by John Catt Educational Ltd

15 Riduna Park, Station Road,
Melton, Woodbridge IP12 1QT
UK
Tel: +44 (0) 1394 389850

4500 140th Ave North,
Suite 101, Clearwater,
FL 33762-3848
US
Tel: +1 561 448 1987

Email: enquiries@johncatt.com
Website: www.johncatt.com

ISBN: 978 1 915261 02 1

Set and designed by John Catt Educational Limited

CONTENTS

Editors 5

Introduction 7

Chapter One: School culture and climate 17

1.1 – Positive school culture 17

1.2 – Adult mindsets 19

1.3 – Professional learning 22

1.4 – Safe and supportive climate 26

1.5 – Family engagement 29

Chapter Two: Curriculum 35

2.1 – High-quality, knowledge-rich curriculum 35

2.2 – Reading 38

2.3 – Writing 44

2.4 – Mathematics 48

2.5 – Science and social studies 51

2.6 – Social and emotional learning 54

Chapter Three: Instruction 57

3.1 – Instructional strategies 57

3.2 – Assessing student progress 59

3.3 – Supports for students with disabilities 62

3.4 – Supports for English learners 64

3.5 – Supports for low-income gifted and talented students 66

Chapter Four: Recovering from the pandemic 69

    4.1 – Targeted help and high-dosage tutoring 69

    4.2 – Expanded mental health supports 76

    4.3 – Implementation 85

Appendix: Acknowledgements 89

Annotated bibliography 93

Endnotes 133

EDITORS

Michael J. Petrilli is president of the Thomas B. Fordham Institute, research fellow at Stanford University's Hoover Institution, executive editor of *Education Next*, and a Distinguished Senior Fellow for Education Commission of the States. An award-winning writer, he is the author of *The Diverse Schools Dilemma*, editor of *Education for Upward Mobility*, and co-editor of *How to Educate an American*. Petrilli has published opinion pieces in the *New York Times*, *Washington Post*, *Wall Street Journal*, *Bloomberg*, and *Slate*, and appears  frequently on television and radio. Petrilli helped to create the US Department of Education's Office of Innovation and Improvement and the Policy Innovators in Education Network. He serves on the advisory boards of the Association of American Educators, MDRC, and the National Association of Charter School Authorizers. He lives with his family in Bethesda, Maryland.

Barbara Davidson is a former classroom teacher of learning-disabled students who has worked for the past 35 years to advance three levers for producing K–12 academic improvements: the role that high-quality curriculum plays in supporting teacher excellence, the importance of building students' background knowledge of the world as a strategy for reading success, and the octane that specific evidence-based instructional practices can provide for learning.  Barbara runs StandardsWork (www.standardswork. org), a national nonprofit that promotes research on the "curriculum effect" and elevates both educator and family voices in support of a curriculum renaissance. She also serves as Executive Director of the Knowledge Matters

Campaign (www.knowledgematterscampaign.org) which, among other things, sponsors the Knowledge Matters School Tour designed to "find the good and praise" districts that are utilizing these three levers to change outcomes for students.

Kathleen Carroll is longtime education journalist and manuscript editor at *Education Next*. Her longform, data-driven reporting has won top prizes from the Education Writers Association, Annie E. Casey Foundation, and Investigative Reporters and Editors, among others. She has more than two decades of experience in strategic storytelling and analysis, including as publications editor at TNTP. She frequently partners with leading foundations, researchers, and practitioners to explain the ideas and innovations that  advance opportunity for students across the economic spectrum. kathcarroll.com

INTRODUCTION

"Follow the science."

Those three words became a rallying cry during the Covid pandemic. And at first blush, the message seems straightforward: identify best practice according to the evidence, and then do it.

But it's not quite that simple in the real world, whether the subject is how to respond to a deadly virus, how to educate our children, or how to do both at the same time.

The first challenge is defining "the science." As Jonathan Rauch of the Brookings Institution explains in his recent book, *The Constitution of Knowledge*, science is no stationary thing.[1] It is constantly changing, as researchers publish fresh studies and new bits of knowledge are added to the old, and as old understandings are overtaken by new ones. We certainly saw this with the pandemic, as we learned over time how the novel coronavirus was transmitted (by air, not on surfaces), and thus how best to mitigate its spread (by avoiding poorly ventilated and crowded spaces, not by constant deep cleaning).

It's also clear that "the science" is constantly contested, both by scientists and the larger public. That's actually the essence of science: no one gets the exclusive right to claim what the evidence says, much less a permanent right to do so. As Rauch argues, the scientific endeavor is, by its very nature, a social exercise. It's a process; a conversation. A community of informed individuals argues and debates until something approaching a consensus emerges, and then they start again. That's why we need to "follow" the science—it keeps moving, it's never static.

Following the science is seldom easy, especially in the realm of education. What science did we follow when we shifted American schools to remote learning in March 2020 and, for many schools, continued that well into the 2020-21 school year? While keeping kids at home reduced the spread of Covid, this decision also had an enormous negative impact on many students' academic achievement and mental health. As experiences mount and evidence grows, our understanding grows more complex. Following the science involves trade-offs, value judgments, and the complications, compromises, and tough choices endemic in the real world.

Yet for all of its limitations and complexities, "following the science" is one of the primary ways that we humans have made progress over the centuries. It has allowed us to solve problems at a global scale and brought us lifesaving vaccines to counter Covid in less than a year. It is why drinking water in the developed world is almost always clean, why farms can feed billions, why infant mortality has plummeted and life spans have expanded in ways that our ancestors could have never imagined. And it is why we live with advanced technologies and living standards for the masses that surpass those of kings and queens of yesteryear.

"Following the science" is also one of the primary ways that we can improve our schools so that all American children finally gain the opportunity to fulfill their potential and thrive in the world they will inherit. The urgency of this goal only grew during the pandemic, which cruelly disrupted the home and school lives of children around the world.

Our hope with this book is to identify what the science tells us about evidence-based practices in elementary schools and, based on the experiences of highly effective elementary schools, describe what this looks like in the real world of classrooms. Following the science into its application in this way—and sharing how it works on the ground—enables us to suggest workable answers to key questions rather than challenging every teacher, school, or district, to figure out those answers on their own.

We're talking here about the fundamental questions of elementary education, such as:

- How can young children make sense of the code that is the alphabet? How can we help them move smoothly from sounding out words to reading fluently and confidently?

- How does "reading comprehension" develop? Is it a skill to be learned? Or is it more like a process—driven by how much students know about the world via subjects like history and geography and science?

- How can elementary students be taught to write effectively? Should we worry about spelling, grammar, and punctuation right away, or can that come later? How can we teach children to write strong sentences, paragraphs, and essays?

- What about math? Should we simply teach kids to memorize $9 + 6 = 15$ or is there a phase when it's better to show them various strategies to figure out and understand why 9 and 6 add up to 15? Are there some ways to teach fractions that work better than others?
- Should we place students in small groups with peers at their same level in reading, writing, or math, or should we mix it up?
- Should students practice reading skills with books at their current reading level or at one that corresponds to their assigned school grade (and above)?
- How do we help low-achieving and high-achieving students both make as much progress as possible?
- What's the appropriate role of homework?
- How should teachers manage their classrooms? What's the best way to keep an orderly, yet friendly, environment?

Let's get one thing clear right away: not everything that makes an elementary school great can be pinned to "evidence." Great teaching and inspired leadership are an art *and* a science. And sometimes science can't give us a single strong answer to every question.

But oftentimes, it does. The science is out there. The evidence can point the way. And there are good approaches to meeting the challenges that thousands of teachers and students encounter every day. When the adults in charge ask for evidence and put it into practice, we can do better by our students tomorrow than we did yesterday.

Why elementary education?

If we had to single out the most important institution in civic life, the one with the greatest potential to change a country's course, it would be the humble elementary school. We see four big reasons why.

First, within our education system, we believe these schools have the greatest potential impact on kids' academic, social, and emotional progress. Partly that's just basic math: in America, most children spend almost half of their K–12 careers in elementary schools, usually six out of 13 years. And grades K–5 are also the years when kids tend to learn the most. The average student achievement gains during elementary school far outpace those seen in middle school or high school.

The second reason is the broad consensus, even in polarized times, regarding what elementary schools are supposed to accomplish. At the elementary level, almost everyone agrees that kids should learn to read, write, and do arithmetic, learn to get along with other children, and get a basic grounding in science, music, the arts, and the nation's history and its civic institutions. That's a consensus that's far harder to find when it comes to middle or high schools. Of course, some parents want something more or different for their children. But as we learned when one of us surveyed parents years ago about their educational preferences, the vast majority just want a quality school that teaches kids the basics.[2]

Third, if we could dramatically improve our elementary schools, we would instantly transform our middle and high schools. That's because the greatest challenges in secondary education relate to children who enter ill-prepared—it's hard to build on the wobbly foundation of an inadequate elementary education. Alas, even America's very best high-poverty elementary schools don't get all of their students to grade-level academic achievement by the end of the fifth grade. Few even come close, which is why most middle schools have to try and make up for kids coming in two or three grade levels behind. Longtime education analyst Marc Tucker reports that other advanced nations have solved this problem.[3] Imagine what it would mean if we did, too.

The fourth reason to focus on elementary schools is that is where we have the best research evidence about what works—which is to say, the closest thing to consensus and the strongest science to follow.

This is most clearly the case when it comes to reading, where we have decades of research that shows how systemically teaching students phonics and phonemic awareness is an essential step in early literacy development.[4] We are also building a strong evidence base that content knowledge in subjects like history, science, geography, and the arts allows children to develop strong reading comprehension abilities.[5]

But it's not just reading. In math, too, we now understand the importance of mastering basic math facts to automaticity, as well as the imperative of developing computational, conceptual, and problem-solving skills as students progress through the elementary grades.[6] So too on other topics, from classroom management to effective professional learning to the power of small-group tutoring.

To put it bluntly, volumes on evidenced-based practices for middle schools or high schools would be much shorter, and weaker, than the one you hold in your hand!

The challenges ahead

How often have you picked up an education book to read how, according to the authors, the system is broken, failing and flailing—but their ideas for fixing it will bring about a miraculous transformation?

That's not our approach.

Sure, we believe that the American system of education could achieve significantly better results than it has to date. But we also recognize that its schools have gotten better over time—especially elementary schools, and especially for the most disadvantaged students.

Consider this: from the mid- to late 1990s, and generally until 2010, scores on the National Assessment of Educational Progress (NAEP) improved for the lowest-achieving students and Black and Hispanic students in grades 4 and 8. The gains in reading, math, and most other academic subjects were greatest at the low end of the spectrum, with a big drop in the percentage of students scoring at the "below basic" level. By 2010 or so, Black, Hispanic, and low-achieving students were reading and doing math at much higher grade levels than their predecessors in the early 1990s—two and sometimes three years ahead. That's historic, life-changing progress. And it surely contributed to more recent gains in the high school graduation rate for these groups, as many more kids came into ninth grade closer to being on track.

Schools can't take all the credit for these improvements. Economic conditions were also getting better for poor families in the 1990s and beyond—and when that ended, due to the Great Recession of 2008, we saw many more kids in poverty, school budgets slashed, and other enormous headwinds.

Yet it's also clear to us that one explanation for the historic educational gains of not so long ago was the progress our schools were making in "following the science." Especially in early reading and math instruction, we know more about what works than we did in the past, and we see more schools putting that knowledge into practice. Our perspective is that we need to keep at it. We need to accelerate the pace and expand an evidence-based approach to more aspects of the elementary school experience.

What counts as "evidence"?

Yes, it's a genuine challenge. If we set our evidentiary standards impossibly high and look only to gold-standard experimental studies, we risk limiting ourselves to questions that lend themselves to randomization or to practices, tools, and materials that have been on the market long enough (and have enough financial backing) to allow for robust, expensive evaluations. But if we set our standards too low, we risk encouraging practices that may look "promising" but might be ineffective—or even harmful.

Our approach is to turn to the core tenets of science that have served us well, in all fields, for hundreds of years. In Rauch's words, those "rules for reality" are:

- **The fallibilist rule: no one gets the final say.** You may claim that a statement is established as knowledge only if it can be debunked, in principle, and only insofar as it withstands attempts to debunk it.

- **The empirical rule: no one has personal authority.** You may claim that a statement has been established as knowledge only insofar as the method used to check it gives the same result regardless of the identity of the checker, and regardless of the source of the statement.[7]

These rules mean that people can't just make stuff up or claim that certain practices are "evidence-based" just because someone said they are. But they also leave room for many different approaches to identify plausible practices and test them against the rigors of the real world. And they certainly mean going beyond randomized experiments.

For example, in this book we will point to rigorous analyses that examine whether particular instructional materials are faithful to evidence-based practices that themselves have been validated by experimental studies. This approach is several steps removed from subjecting the instructional materials themselves to controlled experiments, but we think that's OK. Likewise, we will laud rigorous attempts to chronicle what high-performing schools and highly effective teachers do in their classrooms, most famously the work of Doug Lemov and his colleagues on the *Teach Like a Champion* team.

We believe this approach is in line with the one embraced by the US Congress in the Every Student Succeeds Act of 2015. That law mentions the term "evidence-based practice" over 100 times, and defines the term via four tiers: strong, moderate, promising, and "under evaluation."

And we will be transparent with you, our reader, about the strength (or fragility) of the research.

Keeping track of a moving target

Our goal in these pages, then, is to apply reasonable standards of evidence to the mountains of studies, evaluations, white papers, and advertising pitches that land every week on the desks of state and district administrators, elementary school principals, and teachers.

But let's be honest: we can't claim to read every single word that is published on the topic of elementary school practices. Nobody could. We had to take shortcuts, mostly by relying on other rigorous syntheses of the research.

Resources produced by the US Department of Education's Institute for Education Sciences (IES)—especially its collection of practice guides and reviews by the What Works Clearinghouse (WWC)—have been especially helpful. Launched in 2003, the WWC is a repository of evidence for "what works" in education. In addition to setting standards for what is (and isn't) considered high-quality research, the WWC examines existing research on "programs, products, practices, and policies in education" and issues reviews and "intervention reports," all in a highly searchable database.

Since 2007, the WWC has also produced 24 practice guides, which summarize the findings and recommendations of expert panels about the literature, such as *Organizing Instruction and Study to Improve Learning*, or *Teaching Math to Young Children*.[8] These practice guides attempt to codify the science when it comes to K–12 education. They form the backbone of our recommendations.

But we didn't stop with the WWC. Also exceptionally helpful in our quest was the Annenberg Institute's EdResearch for Recovery series, a set of short briefs for practitioners on topics that are particularly timely in the aftermath of the pandemic, as well as the "Evidence for ESSA" collection of reviews of K–12 programs published by Johns Hopkins University.

In this effort, we are not trying to break new ground. We are not researchers ourselves, but lifelong consumers of research; people who have long been interested in the promise of evidence-based education. This book is a comprehensive attempt to scour the highest quality resources and syntheses of evidence out there and communicate their findings with user-friendly language, with an understanding of the real-world complexities of schools and classrooms.

It is our sincere hope that this book's first edition will not be its last. The research base will continue to evolve, and so too should this volume.

Indeed, this venture started as a crowdsourced document placed on a dynamic wiki. It would not have been possible without the efforts of multiple educators, academics, and other experts. The first draft was written with loving care by Barbara Davidson and Greg Woodward. That early draft was road-tested and readied for wide circulation after feedback from several staff members at the Thomas B. Fordham Institute, including Chester E. Finn Jr., Amber M.

Northern, Robert Pondiscio, David Griffith, Chad Aldis, Victoria McDougald, Julie Fitz, and Melissa Gutwein. We solicited and responded to in-depth comments from more than three dozen instructional leaders, scholars, and other experts, who you'll find listed in the appendix. Kathleen Carroll took this feedback and masterfully knitted it into a much stronger draft. Once the wiki went live, additional practitioners from across the US provided constructive feedback, leading to a second version of the document, called *The Acceleration Imperative* and available at www.CAOCentral.org. Fordham's Brandon Wright continued to make significant improvements to the text as the content was serialized on Fordham's *Flypaper* blog, and Fordham's Pedro Enamorado did a marvelous job helping us turn the wiki into a book.

We cannot thank our reviewers enough for their insights and improvements. Together, they have recommended more than 1000 changes to our document to date. That's the spirit of the evidence-based enterprise: it's a group effort, and the bigger the circle of academics and practitioners sharing their knowledge and experience about what works, the faster and stronger our outcomes will be.

Curriculum is key

A constant drumbeat in these pages is the importance of high-quality instructional materials. We do not believe it makes sense for each one of America's teachers or principals, or even chief academic officers at the district or charter network level, to try to interpret the research evidence on their own. Such an approach would be isolating, time-consuming, costly, and inefficient.

Instead, we believe that instructional materials are the ideal vehicle for turning evidence into practice. Curriculum developers—with insights from academics and practitioners—should develop evidence-based resources designed for the reality of the classroom, so educators can put them to their best purpose. We don't have to be computer engineers in order to use computers effectively in our daily work. Likewise, teachers shouldn't have to earn doctorates in education research in order to teach children effectively. If developers do their job well, then educators can focus on mastering the curriculum, rather than learning every intricacy of the underlying research studies.

Simply put, we think it is almost impossible to be an evidence-based elementary school without the adoption and implementation of high-quality instructional materials. Educators need tools that are aligned with the research, and quality instructional materials are the most critical of those tools.

Our vision for elementary education

The foremost job of elementary schools is to prepare students to succeed in middle school and beyond. That means their major focus should be on the development of academic skills and knowledge, as well as the social and emotional skills that contribute to success in school and in life.

But that doesn't mean we dream of Dickensian education factories with "drill and kill" instruction and drill-sergeant discipline. Great elementary schools are joyful places, alive with wonder and a strong sense of mission, where relationships and curiosity flourish. There's nothing about evidence-based practices that needs to imply a tension with what so many educators love about elementary schools, and the brilliant and beautiful children they serve.

In the wake of a horrific pandemic, even the best elementary schools are struggling to help their students make up for lost time, relearn forgotten skills, and get their momentum back again. You'll find lots of ideas in this book, especially in the last section, about how we can help young children recover, regain, and thrive.

Enough with the preliminaries. Let's dive in!

CHAPTER ONE
SCHOOL CULTURE AND CLIMATE

1.1 – POSITIVE SCHOOL CULTURE

In schools with positive cultures, adults share clearly articulated values and beliefs, work purposefully together, and follow well-established norms to meet a common set of high expectations for teaching and learning.

The values and beliefs that a school community puts into practice each day define its culture. Schools with positive cultures have shared narratives, habits of mind, and effective ways of getting things done. They have articulated a coherent vision for excellence and can draw on that to flexibly respond to challenges, craft solutions, and reinforce practices that promote student success.

The conditions that support such cultures are influenced by the school's climate—a distinct but related quality that determines the mood and feeling of a school community, the nature of relationships among adults and students, and expectations for physical and emotional security (see *1.4 – Safe and supportive climate* for more).

The fast-moving changes and interruptions in schooling caused by the pandemic have highlighted the importance of maintaining a positive school culture. Systems and networks that had established shared beliefs and norms prior to the crisis had more tools to help in their response and recovery. Schools that entered the crisis without aligned structures and values in place were at a disadvantage that was only compounded by the inequities that accompanied remote learning in high-poverty areas.

School culture includes many interrelated parts and can be difficult to define and change. But that will be a critical task to a productive pandemic recovery. School leaders must assess the routine practices of teachers, staff, students, and parents, identify the values and beliefs that drive those practices, and create the conditions for long-term success.

Recommendations

- Administer a school culture survey to evaluate the current strengths and weaknesses across the community, such as those from Johns Hopkins University (which also assesses climate more broadly) and UChicago Impact.[9] Do teachers and staff view the school as having clear, high expectations for teaching and learning? Do they feel that vision is aligned with school or network policies and practices?

- Work with senior leaders in your school community, including parents and teachers, to ensure a clear articulation of the school's mission and values, and use that mission and vision statement to model actions and drive decision-making related to the pandemic and beyond.

- Conduct an audit of school practices, including curriculum implementation and scaffolding, teacher professional development, disciplinary codes, grading policies, and awards ceremonies, to ensure a through-line from the school's mission to its institutional practices.

- Facilitate teacher leadership and collaboration to reinforce and share ownership of the school's mission and vision.[10] Providing more opportunities for staff to communicate directly with one another helps beliefs, values, and aligned actions take root and become stable norms.

Rationale

A strong and positive school culture is characterized by a clear sense of direction and shared accountability to advance a vision for success, which shapes how teachers and leaders do their jobs. It is built on mutual respect and trust, which are the foundation of learning communities.[11]

Scholars have identified the power of coherent culture in successful schools of all types. For example, a study of high-performing Catholic high schools attributed their impact on students to several aspects of school culture, including a decentralized structure that prioritized decision-making and leadership at the school level and a clear, common understanding of what all students should learn.[12] Scott Seider's exploration of how three Boston charter schools prioritize character development shows the impact of strong school culture as well as social and emotional learning.[13] And Karin Chenoweth's book looking at how beliefs and aligned practices support academic achievement in high-poverty district schools provides another distinct source of examples of school culture at work.[14]

Positive school cultures have already supported some early responses to the pandemic. For example, a consortium of high-performing charter schools drew on their earlier reform work and professional collaborations to create the National Summer School Initiative (now Cadence Learning).[15] Guilford County Schools, an innovative North Carolina district that has run its own teacher-licensing program since 2008, enlisted its master teachers to build an online library of instructional videos, a natural extension of its teacher-leadership Opportunity Culture initiative.[16]

We note here that a strong culture cannot take root or thrive without a healthy school climate, and the values and actions that support these dimensions tend to go hand in hand. Schools must be safe from violence, both for students and teachers. Students from different socioeconomic, racial, or ethnic backgrounds should feel equally at home.[17] Schools must support students' emotional and social needs, while families must feel and actually be included as important members of the school community.[18] Teachers must be respected by their principals, given the tools to lead rigorous classrooms, and be provided with opportunities to lead and collaborate with one another.

1.2 – ADULT MINDSETS

Adult mindsets are the beliefs and expectations about student achievement that influence school culture, drive decision-making, and accelerate or hinder student success.

Student outcomes are strongly linked to adult mindsets, and teachers and leaders at high-performing schools tend to share a common set of high expectations for success.[19] That's always been true, but may be more important than ever given the challenges created by the pandemic. Many students are contending with massive learning losses and emotional trauma, and caring adults may be inclined, even in subtle ways, to lower the bar and shield students from challenging work.

While educators should certainly demonstrate empathy, it's essential that adult expectations for student progress remain high—among educators and parents alike.[20] At school, instructional materials, teaching methods, teacher–student interactions, grading practices, and professional learning experiences should ensure mechanisms for expressing high expectations are in place. They also should identify and build on the strengths and assets students bring with them from their homes and communities, and emphasize student agency, growth mindset, and other "soft skills" that can support thriving futures.

School culture should push back against the soft bigotry of low expectations—including bias related to race and class—and support students to set and achieve ambitious goals.[21]

Recommendations

- Articulate shared high expectations for student engagement, work, and mastery across the school, district, or network. Use common planning time to address current mindsets, assumptions, beliefs, biases, and prejudices that may influence staff's ability to set and hold students to high expectations as the school focuses on recovery.

- Select high-quality instructional materials embedded with high expectations (see *2.1 – High-quality, knowledge-rich curriculum* for more).

- Implement a school-wide approach to grading student work to ensure consistently high standards that are tied to exemplar student assignments (such as EL Education's Models of Excellence), and establish rubrics and grading scales and common policies for accepting late assignments.

- Implement a school-wide approach to managing student behavior (see *1.4 – Safe and supportive climate* for more).

- Administer student surveys to uncover the extent to which students believe that teachers hold high academic expectations for them. Survey instruments to consider include those from Tripod or Panorama Education.

- When hiring for teacher vacancies, look for teachers with a record of high expectations for children, and especially children of color. Given the studies showing that teachers of color tend to hold higher expectations for students of color, prioritize teacher diversity in hiring decisions as well.

Rationale

Teachers hold often unspoken beliefs about who they and their students are and what they both can do, and research shows that those mindsets matter.[22] Several studies have found that students recognize when teachers hold high expectations for them and perform better academically when they do. Conversely, when teachers hold differentiated expectations for students, as opposed to uniformly high expectations for all students, these low expectations are correlated with lower academic achievement.

Tragically, some studies have found that teachers tend to have lower expectations for students of color; helping teachers see their own implicit racial biases and working to counteract them is essential.[23] It is critical to discuss and recognize the difference between holding all students accountable to high expectations for learning and using high expectations to further inequitable practices and uphold inequitable or racist policies and practices. Research by David M. Quinn shows bias is pervasive in school grading, and research by Travis Riddle and Stacey Sinclair finds evidence of bias in discipline practices, for example. A rigorous approach to culturally responsive teaching also can support high expectations for all.[24]

One of the best ways to ensure that a culture of high expectations is in place is via the adoption and faithful implementation of high-quality instructional materials (see *2.1 – High-quality, knowledge-rich curriculum* for more). Explicit support for teachers to understand and use these materials as designed is critical. Often, when teachers encounter a new, high-quality curriculum, they worry that it is too difficult for their students and substitute simpler content and instruction, which limits learning. When students are given lower-level reading assignments or less demanding discussion prompts, for example, it becomes impossible for them to catch up to grade-level expectations.

The best instructional materials are designed to give all students access to the same challenging content, including through robust scaffolds embedded to support student learning for students who do not possess the prerequisite concepts or skills. These materials also include professional development support for teachers, including opportunities to revisit their expectations and practice rigorous new instruction in professional learning communities (see *1.3 – Professional learning* for more). Such a supported shift to more demanding content and instruction makes it possible for all students to master grade-level standards.

Connecting mindsets and materials to classroom practice is the next step. High-performing charter networks call this "intellectual prep."[25] They use teachers' common planning time to review curriculum and evidence of student progress, establish common expectations and grading norms, and ensure lessons leave the heavy lifting to students, through productive struggling with rigorous, grade-level content. For example, the charter-school networks Achievement First, Uncommon Schools, and Success Academy have taken this approach to set the stage for high expectations.[26]

In addition, educators who model holding high expectations for all can inspire a "growth mindset," which can positively influence student performance in school. A recent study by the OECD found that students with a strong growth mindset scored significantly higher on the Program for International Student

Assessment (PISA) in all subjects—32 points in reading and 23 points in math.[27] In the United States, having a growth mindset was associated with a 60-point higher score in reading, compared to the scores of students who believe intelligence is fixed.

Many of the highest performing, high-poverty schools embrace specific pedagogical practices that convey high expectations, such as those identified by Doug Lemov in his highly influential book, *Teach Like a Champion*.[28] These include four major techniques.

Technique	Technique description	How it promotes high expectations
No Opt Out	Students are held accountable to always make an effort	Students practice answering challenging questions and know that their teachers are not giving up on them
Right is Right	Partially correct answers from students are not "rounded up" to fully correct	Students receive the message that they are capable of getting an answer completely right
Stretch It	OK/good verbal and written answers from students are pushed to be more robust	Students are pushed to expand on "B" answers to make them "A" answers
Without Apology	The teacher does not ever apologize for the material being challenging	The students never hear from the teacher that something is too hard for them

1.3 – PROFESSIONAL LEARNING

Professional learning is an ongoing process in which teachers study, probe, and practice new instructional techniques, investigate curriculum, and collaborate with colleagues to enhance content knowledge and pedagogical skills.

Ongoing professional learning for educators that is well designed, based on the science of learning, responsive to teachers' needs, and aligned with school-wide priorities is the bedrock of positive school culture. There's simply no way any school can implement high-quality curricula and research-based instructional practices, or address students' unfinished learning and mental health needs, without it.

Most professional learning should be tied directly to the high-quality curriculum a school, district, or network has chosen—including time for teachers to read the passages their students will read and practice the math exercises they will assign in class. Administrators also should schedule frequent opportunities for observation and feedback on teachers' instructional practice by peers, coaches, and school leaders, using established frameworks and grade-level expectations for student achievement. In addition, during shared professional learning time in subject or grade-level groups, teachers should focus on developing deep content and curriculum knowledge, by studying curriculum, planning and practicing lessons, and carefully examining student work.

Recommendations

- Link professional learning and curriculum work together. When purchasing or procuring curriculum, also arrange for professional development services from the curriculum developer or from an expert training organization that specializes in supporting educators to use that curriculum. Our contributors and reviewers point to leading organizations such as SchoolKit, Teaching Lab, Instruction Partners, TNTP, and Leading Educators. Rivet Education is a trusted source of reviews for professional learning providers.

- Many schools have professional learning communities (PLCs) on the books, but these structures and times are not always well used. Avoid "PLC Lite" by building regular PLC time into the weekly schedule (see 4.3 – *Implementation* section for more).[29] Provide skilled facilitators to lead those sessions and establish agendas that focus on curriculum study and candid discussions of student progress, including detailed reviews of work samples and data analysis. Districts can build on new technological expertise to establish more focused PLCs, such as by grouping teachers across schools, or giving teachers regular access to a content specialist during virtual meetings.

- Schedule time for teachers and instructional coaches to observe other teachers or watch videos of their lessons, and offer feedback, and normalize that as part of grade-level PLC work. In particular, coaches or PLC facilitators should ask questions and push teachers to think deeply about their instruction and impact on student learning. For schools shifting to new curriculum, this should take the form of intellectual prep, which focuses on the major ideas and exemplar student responses in a target lesson.[30]

- Ensure school or district leadership and decision-making is aligned to goals for ongoing professional learning and curriculum implementation. This could mean reassigning a staff member to handle oversight, or partnering with an external professional learning vendor to support change management, provide leadership development, or troubleshoot logistics. In all cases, maintaining a coherent approach to professional learning, using the school's curriculum as a guide, is key.

Rationale

Components of strong professional learning

Strong professional learning focuses on what Richard Elmore terms the "instructional core": the relationship between the content, teacher, and student. Each component of the core affects the others.[31] To improve student learning at scale, schools can raise the level of the content that students are taught, increase the skill and knowledge that teachers bring to the teaching of that content, and increase the level of students' active learning of the content. This framework establishes the imperative of putting *what happens in the classroom* at the very center of professional development efforts.

When a school has a high-quality curriculum to focus on, it also has a north star for professional learning. High-quality curriculum supports a teacher's content knowledge and pedagogical skill, builds on the science of learning to present content and activities in a coherent way, and clarifies expectations for teaching and learning. Professional learning should focus on the ways the curriculum teaches certain content. Why does the curriculum emphasize certain skills or ideas? Why is it structured how it is? How can it be effectively implemented and scaffolded? This is in addition to mastering effective classroom practices and studying the learning science that underlies strong curriculum and instruction.

Given the infinite array of possible outcomes to any given lesson—which vary with each student's level of preparation, how they are doing on a given day, what's going on in the world around them, and so forth—teaching is ultimately a series of hundreds of granular decisions about execution and response. Curriculum-based professional learning focuses those decisions and helps to ensure that, over time, they are made with increased intentionality and consistency.

It's important to note that this does not all happen over a summer; rather, it is the result of sustained work over time and requires aligned district and school leadership, the buy-in of union representatives, and stability at the school board and superintendent levels.

Another vitally important feature of effective professional learning and schools is the prioritization of time for intentionally structured PLCs. Numerous studies document teacher-perceived benefits of PLCs, and some also demonstrate positive student outcomes, including increases in academic achievement.[32] By far the most compelling use and rationale for PLCs is the opportunity for teachers to collaboratively interrogate and intellectually prepare to teach the curriculum, as well as identify what is (or is not) working and why. PLC structures also can support observations by peers or instructional coaches. This is akin to the Japanese lesson study, which provides teachers with the opportunity to plan, teach, observe, and critique their practice with colleagues.[33]

Some districts and networks can serve as examples of this approach to curriculum-based, collaborative professional learning. For example, under the LEAP program at DC Public Schools, teachers meet weekly with trained leaders to unpack and rehearse lessons from the district's Common Core-aligned curriculum and are regularly observed and given feedback from an instructional coach.[34] Other examples and resources include IDEA Public Schools Days of Practice; Achievement First's intellectual prep and unit unpacking protocols; EL Education's protocols for studying the quality of student work; and Uncommon Schools' Practice Perfect.[35]

Research review

The evidence base for curriculum-based professional learning is nascent, and more research is needed. But there is a strong base of research supporting our professional learning recommendations.

In a 2009 article, Thomas Guskey and Kwang Suk Yoon summarized findings from more than 1300 studies that looked at impacts of professional development on student learning.[36] The research indicated several characteristics of effective efforts. These include a focus on content, with activities that "were designed to help teachers better understand both what they teach and how students acquire specific content knowledge and skill," and on careful adaptation of varied instructional practices rather than a single set of "best practices." Effective development also involves outside experts, without whom teachers tended to focus on practices they already considered effective, rather than those shown to produce results. They also found evidence that workshops are not necessarily ineffective, and that follow-up is crucial to success.

In addition, a 2017 research brief by Linda Darling-Hammond, published by the Learning Policy Institute, cites seven features of effective professional development, based on a review of 35 studies over the last three decades:[37]

1. Content focused.
2. Incorporates active learning using adult learning theory.
3. Supports collaboration, typically in job-embedded contexts.
4. Uses models and modeling of effective practice.

5. Provides coaching and expert support.

6. Offers opportunities for feedback and reflection.

7. Is of sustained duration.

The Carnegie Corporation of New York recently released a challenge paper about the importance of curriculum-based professional learning that builds on this research.[38] It calls for decision-makers at the system and school levels, curriculum designers, professional learning facilitators, and school-based personnel to begin to align their systems around such a vision. Louisiana, for example, has taken a curriculum-oriented approach to teacher learning and created open-source curriculum and aligned professional-learning resources.[39]

Transformative professional learning promotes a high level of cognitive dissonance, disturbs teachers' equilibrium, and must include the time and support they need to reflect on and revise their thinking. Teachers often sit with cognitive dissonance and stay attached to their belief rather than reality. With leaders' support, and in a culture of trust and safety, teachers can take the risks needed to grapple with this dissonance.[40] They can disrupt their assumptions and gain new evidence about what works through using new curriculum materials. That can prompt changes in practice and ultimately, in underlying beliefs.

Our bet is that this type of "transformative professional learning" is a defining characteristic of effective elementary schools, based on the strength of the arguments for high-quality, content-rich curriculum. It can support teachers as they develop mastery with that curriculum and ensure that school leaders and outside experts "walk the walk" as they lead their team.

1.4 – SAFE AND SUPPORTIVE CLIMATE

In a safe and supportive climate, students and adults maintain caring, trusting relationships that promote mutual respect, physical and emotional security, and productive teaching and learning.

Feeling safe and valued is vital to a child's development. Learning suffers when students fear for their safety, worry about being bullied, or don't sense their teachers have high expectations for their success. In a healthy, supportive climate, students are engaged and take intellectual risks. They follow well-established rules and norms for behavior that their teachers and school leaders model and maintain. Such a community is characterized by positive relationships between teachers and students, a place where genuine respect is the norm, and where all students feel they belong.

The same is true for adults—both the teachers and families who make up a school community. In a nurturing climate, educators and family members share candid exchanges based on mutual interests and respect. Their social and emotional needs are part of the equation.

This climate does not occur magically—rather, it must be cultivated through deliberate school-wide strategies, expectations, and rules. A safe and supportive climate should reflect shared values and take into account the communities and cultures students bring with them to school. And it must include sound classroom-management practices and developmentally appropriate supports, including social wellbeing and mental health interventions. This will be particularly important—and challenging—in the post-pandemic era, given the significant trauma so many students likely experienced over the past year, especially those growing up in poverty.

Recommendations

- Establish and maintain authentic, candid relationships with students and their families that reflect and show respect for their communities and cultures. In-school actions like greeting individual students by name and making time for regular check-in conversations can be helpful, as can family-outreach strategies like calling home to share a positive report from a school day or surveying parents on their opinions of the school (see *1.5 – Family engagement* for more on this). Positive relationships and sustaining connections don't just come from clear and consistent expectations—they require explicit attention, and can be data-informed just as academic content instruction can be.

- Uphold a consistent, shared code of conduct in which students and adults are expected to work hard, show respect for the rules and one another, and make positive behavioral choices. Focus efforts on preventing disruption, including through recognizing and rewarding positive behavior and providing mental health supports for students who have experienced trauma and may struggle with self-regulation (see *4.2 – Expanded mental health supports* section for more).[41]

- Set and communicate high expectations for all students and provide access to these goals through universal supports, such as after-school office hours or tutoring that is open to all.

- Guard against racially biased discipline, including by carefully tracking and analyzing data on misbehavior and the school's response, including office referrals and in- or out-of-school suspensions.

- Consider assigning instructional duties by subject-area strength or "looping" students so they work with the same teacher for more than one year.
- Adopt practices that support teachers' emotional wellbeing, such as informal socializing, regular check-ins, and limits on evening emails.[42]

Rationale

Positive relationships between students and teachers are at the core of a successful classroom environment, one where students feel seen, work hard, and treat one another with respect. We know that when there are such relationships, students are happier and more likely to thrive, and point to work such as Lisa Delpit's concept of "warm demanders" and Zaretta Hammond's writing on culturally responsive teaching and neuroscience.[43] A positive school climate is correlated with beneficial student outcomes on many measures, including attendance, assessment outcomes, high-school graduation rates, physical health, and adolescent pro-civic behaviors.[44]

But it is important to understand that strong relationships don't mean friendship-like bonds or generic feelings of being liked. Students respond positively when they know they have a teacher who cares about their success—however that is manifested—rather than knowing they have a teacher who "likes" them. The Search Institute's Developmental Relationships Framework provides a sound model of 20 actions based on five elements: express care, challenge growth, express support, share power, and expand possibilities.[45] In this understanding of climate, teachers don't just "like" their students, they envision and communicate ambitious possibilities for their futures and provide the challenges and supports needed to realize that potential.

This all rests on skillful classroom management, which minimizes disruption and sets clear rules and expectations for behavior and success.[46] Students feel safer and behave better when they know that there are transparent norms in the classroom, and when they know what the consequences will be if they make a mistake.

The National Council on Teacher Quality, in its overview of the research, stresses that positive relationships are developed not through friendship but through a teacher's implementation of "fair rules and productive routines."[47] In other words, teachers need to create a structured, positive environment for students in order for the relationship to be a positive one. Concrete strategies for classroom teachers can be found in *Reducing Behavior Problems in the Elementary School Classroom*, a practice guide published by the Institute of

Education Sciences that affirms the importance of teaching and reinforcing consistent rules and routines, positively reinforcing appropriate behavior, and imposing consequences for negative behavior.[48] Principals and other school leaders should occupy a steady presence in the school's halls and classrooms, which can prevent disciplinary problems from occurring.[49] Critically, teachers and leaders must work to limit bias in disciplinary actions; research has found a connection between implicit bias and disparities in discipline incidents among Black and White students.[50]

The starting point is to ensure that students are highly engaged in learning by choosing high-quality, rigorous curriculum that is content-rich, interesting, and culturally relevant, with instruction that connects *all* students to it. Educators often use the statement "meet students where they are" when thinking about student engagement, which can dilute or reduce the rigor of grade-level work. Instead, we should consider it as a statement that understands exactly "where" the student is. What city do they live in? What about them makes learning relevant? Meaningful learning environments can be both rigorous and culturally relevant and, taken together, make for students who "lean in" from their seats because they are engaged and challenged.

In elementary school classrooms, this tends to mean trading out disconnected literacy skill-building activities like "making inferences" for text-based learning about high-interest topics like the Underground Railroad or explorations in space. Relationships and rules are key, but rich content and effective teaching also help to create orderly and purposeful classroom environments.

Schools with safe and supportive climates also take into account the holistic needs of teachers and students. Engaging, high-quality instruction is key, but so are opportunities for physical activity and unstructured, student-led games and playground time. Daily schedules should have time for exercise outdoors.

1.5 – FAMILY ENGAGEMENT

Family engagement names a core responsibility of a school community: to build partnerships that involve families in a student's education, provide the information and resources that families need to support academic success, and listen to and act on families' needs and wants for their children.

To fully reopen schools and begin to correct for pandemic-related interruptions, students need to reliably attend class and meet expectations for behavior and out-of-school assignments. Many families have been through significant trauma, from illness or losing loved ones, financial hardship, or losing a job or a home. Getting back on track at school will take hard work and focused support both at school and at home.

Family engagement has always been critical to student success, but never more so than now. Schools and families will need to rebuild in-person connections and shore up trust—first, so parents can feel secure in sending children back to school buildings full time, and second, so families can support educators' efforts to accelerate student learning. Some of the digital tools that schools and families have put in place to keep connected over the last year can help. Accessible forms of communication like text messages can build trust and "nudge" families, to the benefit of students.[51]

Recommendations

- Regularly communicate to parents and caregivers expectations for attendance, behavior, and grade-level academic performance—and why these are important factors in children's development and success as adults. These communications should identify the concrete steps the school or district is taking to support students to meet these expectations and make up for pandemic-related learning losses. They also should detail what families can do to support these efforts at home.

- Work to build or rebuild trust at the system level, including by soliciting families' goals for their children and including those goals in program planning. Many of the least-connected parents already distrusted schools even before the pandemic, given their own negative experiences with schools or other institutions. Publicly listening and acting on family priorities is one way to build trust, such as by surveying families and publicly sharing how those responses inform decision-making.

- Open two-way lines of communication between parents and teachers and prioritize staff time to maintain them. Family engagement cannot be seen as something "done" to families. True engagement is mutual and relies on open and frequent communication about what's working and what's not, with students' needs at the center. Successful tactics can include arranging regular "office hours" when families can contact staff for any reason, scheduling regular virtual parent–teacher conferences, and stepped-up outreach efforts by school counselors to check in with families about their needs and expectations.

- Work with community service providers to anticipate and respond flexibly to a variety of family needs, from direct assistance to neighborhood enhancement and mental health support. At the same time, partner with expert organizations to support highly effective instruction using high-quality curricula. In general, efforts to provide knowledge-rich curricula should be complemented by third-party efforts to improve the community environment and expand out-of-school learning opportunities for less advantaged students.[52]

Rationale

School disconnection has played out differently for different families during the pandemic. While some families gained insights as daily instruction played out over Zoom, even the most engaged students have experienced some degree of physical isolation from school environments, and the least engaged students have experienced no schooling at all.

Understanding the cultural factors that shape families' immediate concerns and priorities is important. Schools and families can more easily agree on short-term objectives, like daily attendance, homework, and reading, when they are connected to a shared goal of a meaningful future for students.[53]

A 2016 report by the Pacific Regional Education Lab suggests that two-way communication that includes frequent data sharing with families about children's general academic progress, including both formative and summative assessment scores, has a particularly high impact on students' academic success.[54] These positive impacts are enhanced when schools ask families about students' interests, behaviors, and challenges. For example, a 2019 study out of Germany found evidence that frequent communication between schools and families, wherein schools share data on students' homework completion on a recurrent basis, can increase students' completion of homework assignments.[55] The study found that simply assigning homework without a strong and sustained school–family relationship did not result in high homework completion rates.

Though there is some debate over the value of homework, especially in the younger grades, we know that well-designed, high-quality homework assignments that build on what students are learning in class are beneficial. They also can communicate with parents what their children are learning at school, particularly when teachers review assignments and offer clear feedback. Anecdotal evidence reported in E. D. Hirsch Jr.'s *How to Educate a Citizen* indicates that knowledge-rich curriculum enriches the discussions between parents and their children.[56] Two recent IES practice guides for second-grade teachers and third-grade teachers provide concrete strategies to support families to practice foundational reading skills at home, including evidence-based literacy activities and model language teachers can use to explain how they support student progress.[57]

In addition, reading at home for at least 20 minutes a day has significant academic benefits. A compelling 2020 longitudinal study from the Oxford Review of Education found significant academic benefits correlated with students reading at home, but only when the materials read are books and not other printed materials, such as comics or newspapers.[58] Schools should therefore consider ways to provide low-income families with books.

Finally, both families and schools have a role to play in reducing student absenteeism.[59] A 2007 study from the Mailman School of Public Health at Columbia University points to the devastating academic costs of chronic absenteeism.[60] Chronically absent students score 5% lower, on average, on math and reading standardized assessments compared to their peers.

In short, family engagement should be based on principles of transparency and mutual trust, as articulated in the following delineation of roles and responsibilities:

Core principle	Role of the school	Role of families
Respect for families and their cultures: The heart of family engagement is trust, and that means building real relationships.	Find concrete ways for the principal and classroom teachers to know students, their families, and their cultures.	Participate in school events, both the academically oriented ones like "back-to-school night" and ones intended to build community and celebrate cultures.
Attendance and readiness: Students make the most academic and social-emotional progress when they have enough sleep and are present every day.	Provide rigorous and engaging lessons that start on time every day. Offer social supports to families if attendance and readiness are significant challenges.	To the extent possible, ensure that students get enough sleep and arrive at school on time every day. Take advantage of supports offered by the school to ensure their child's academic success.
Homework: The daily completion of aligned homework assignments supports students' mastery of the school's rigorous curriculum.	Assign meaningful homework assignments that support students' mastery of the curriculum.	Ensure that students complete their homework every day and bring it to school.
Reading: Students need a high-quality curriculum and should read independently for at least 30 minutes every day.	Implement a robust, research-backed ELA curriculum in school and make concrete, low-cost recommendations for literacy-boosting activities and texts to read at home.	Read to young children every day. Ensure that older students read for at least 30 minutes per day.

Core principle	Role of the school	Role of families
Screen time: Excessive screen time can create attention challenges for young children and keeps them from moving their bodies.	Provide concrete, realistic suggestions for how families can set and enforce screen-time limits while children are not at school.	Set and enforce screen-time limits and steer children toward reading, exercise, and play instead.
Active communication: Students' success in school is dependent on parents and teachers routinely and actively communicating with each other.	Share routine academic performance updates with families on at least a weekly basis, in families' preferred languages. Solicit families' feedback via regular, valid, and reliable surveys.	Actively communicate with their child's teacher, including reading all emails and texts that come from the school. Offer feedback proactively or via surveys.

CHAPTER TWO
CURRICULUM

2.1 – HIGH-QUALITY, KNOWLEDGE-RICH CURRICULUM

High-quality, knowledge-rich curriculum thoughtfully sequences content and activities based on the science of learning and provides the materials, tools, and professional learning teachers need to deliver effective instruction.

The faithful implementation of a comprehensive, high-quality curriculum is a necessary (though not sufficient) condition for a high-performing elementary school. High-quality instructional materials shape what students learn, how they engage with content, and how teachers manage their instructional time. Such curricula effectively sequence material for optimal benefit, and the best also incorporate evidence-based practices based on how children learn. A school that has not carefully implemented a high-quality curriculum will struggle to help students address unfinished learning and make sense of the tumultuous events of the last few years.

Recommendations

- Select comprehensive curriculum materials that thoughtfully sequence content and instruction in the four core content areas: English language arts/literacy, mathematics, history/geography, and science (see sections 2.2–2.5 for specific recommendations).
- Base curriculum decisions on college- and career-ready standards and evidence-based instructional practices. Reviews from EdReports are helpful; only green-rated curriculum should be considered.
- Ensure leadership and curriculum implementation is deliberate, intensive, and responsive to teacher feedback. It is not enough to simply

adopt a high-quality curriculum; faithful, ongoing implementation is critical to accelerate student learning. Consider partnering with a support organization such as Instruction Partners, TNTP, or Teaching Lab to ensure fidelity of implementation.

- Ground professional development in the specific content of the curriculum and ensure it explains the research foundation for the curriculum's framework and orientation (see *1.3 – Professional learning* for more).

- Focus on "priority instructional content," as identified by Student Achievement Partners.[61]

- Schedule weekly meetings for grade-level professional learning communities (PLCs) to study the curriculum, examine samples of student work and other data, observe teacher practice, and plan upcoming lessons (see *1.3 – Professional learning* for more).

Rationale

Adopting and implementing a new high-quality, knowledge-based core curriculum is challenging at any time; it will be all the more so in the wake of the pandemic. But for schools, districts, or charter networks currently without one, it will be well worth the effort, as it allows educators to make the best use of instructional time to help students build essential knowledge and skills. In addition, using the same high-quality curriculum across an entire school—or, preferably, an entire district or charter network—can identify and ultimately help prevent gaps in students' knowledge and enable teachers to reliably know what information students already possess as they move from grade to grade.

Schools need to both select and implement new curricula wisely. Decision-makers at schools and districts can investigate possible curricula at EdReports and select among green-rated programs.

In making these decisions, leaders should consider the science of learning—particularly these three elements as described in the 1999 book *How People Learn*:[62]

1. Learning should be based on prior knowledge, and teaching should unearth and clear up misperceptions and help students build on what they already know.

2. A deep base of knowledge distinguishes experts from novices; learning should help students become experts who can retrieve knowledge quickly and apply it to new situations.

3. Metacognition (or thinking about your thinking) should be developed in each area of a curriculum as it helps students take control of their learning.[63]

Evidence shows that changing to a high-quality curriculum can have a strong positive effect on student learning. State-based studies looking at Florida, Indiana, and California have affirmed that the "curriculum effect" is real and particularly large for disadvantaged students.[64] However, David Steiner of Johns Hopkins University raises important questions about what might contribute to curriculum's impact on student learning in a policy brief for StandardsWork.[65] For example, many different types of materials are described as "curriculum" and the selection and implementation of curricula vary widely, so the exact drivers have not yet been precisely defined.

In addition, teachers often supplement curriculum materials with resources available for download online, such as those shared on the Teachers Pay Teachers and Share My Lesson websites. In 2020's "The Supplemental Curriculum Bazaar: Is What's Online Any Good?" a team of reviewers looked at ELA resources from these sites and rated them as mostly mediocre—or worse.[66] While teachers are understandably eager to capitalize on new resources, it's important that what they bring into the classroom is of high quality.

Instructional leaders must play a central role in curriculum implementation. Teachers or schools should not have to individually determine which portions of a textbook need greater emphasis or where key ideas may be missing or provide insufficient student practice. An experienced teacher whose students are demonstrating high levels of success may have earned the right to modify curriculum as needed in certain ways, and schools should be prepared to treat and support a first-year teacher differently than a sixth-year master teacher. But on the whole, teachers should be supported to use well-designed, high-quality curricula with fidelity to the program design. This can free their time and energy to practice and refine instruction, since they are no longer urged or expected to essentially design their own lessons. Few teachers have the time or the training to do that well.

Central offices can alert teachers to likely areas of unfinished learning and provide advice on where and when to bring in additional resources without compromising the coherence of a curriculum. These could include videos, instructional strategies, or professional development specific to a school or district challenge in order to engage all students in grade-level learning and meet specific expectations for the end of the school year. The curriculum should serve as a bedrock of professional learning for teachers, and the lens through which continuous improvement in practice is both inspired and measured (see *1.3 – Professional learning* for more).

Such coherence is key. One study spanning 6000 schools and six states did not find positive effects from implementing high-quality instructional materials, perhaps because of the absence of high-quality instructional supports.[67] Other studies have found that more than half of the possible impact of shifting to a stronger curriculum is lost if the transition does not include development supports to shift teacher practice in a way that specifically supports the new materials.[68] High-quality instructional materials must be used rather than left on the shelf if they are to have a positive impact.

2.2 – READING

A high-quality reading curriculum is based on research and comprehension, and features both components of a strong program of study: an explicit and systematic approach to foundational skills instruction and rich opportunities for vocabulary development and exposure to academic content.

Literacy is the bedrock of every elementary school and should be the top priority for post-pandemic educational recovery. Students are likely to have significant gaps in reading skills and preparation, and educators must be ready to support and accelerate them over the next few years. Federal stimulus funding can help schools implement high-quality curricula and aligned professional learning, expand tutoring, and implement research-based interventions explored in this section.

A high-quality elementary curriculum imparts essential foundational skills in early reading and uses rich, engaging, and culturally responsive literary and informational texts. This allows students to build background knowledge of the world as they learn to read and draw meaning from print—a critical component of literacy instruction. Students need systematic foundational skills instruction, as well as a strong vocabulary and wide exposure to academic content.

However, selecting such curricula can be difficult, as research identifying the effectiveness of specific programs is fraught with challenges. For example, the fidelity of implementation varies and comparisons with control groups are hard to come by. Still, the best English language arts (ELA) curricula embed practices that have been validated by rigorous research and are grounded in the science of reading. In addition, independent curriculum reviews such as those by EdReports, which rate quality based on alignment to college- and career-ready standards, can provide important information about a variety of programs.

In the discussion below, we focus on three considerations for elementary ELA curriculum selection and implementation: the science of reading, standards alignment, and design that gives all students access to grade-level content. We explain how this can be done and explore how these high-impact elements play out in an exemplar curriculum from EL Education.

Recommendations

- Select and implement a high-quality, comprehensive curriculum that is grounded in the science of reading, rich in content, rigorous, culturally relevant, and includes strong teacher-facing materials. We are particularly fond of EL Education, which has earned high ratings from EdReports in grades K–8 and was found effective in a 2013 Mathematica study.[69]

- Give all students the good stuff—appropriately complex texts that align to grade-level standards, by providing struggling readers with the necessary scaffolding and supports.

- Invest staff in the adoption and roll out of new curricula, including any modifications needed to address learning loss.

- Build in regular time for teachers to engage in curriculum study as part of collaborative planning and professional learning.

Rationale

The science of reading

The "science of reading" is a relatively new buzz phrase for a body of research that has existed for decades. In 2000, the National Reading Panel reviewed the evidence and identified five elements of effective reading instruction: phonemic awareness, phonics skills, fluency, vocabulary, and comprehension.[70]

Despite the panel's clear consensus that systematic instruction in phonemic awareness and phonics for all children was the most effective approach to teaching word-level reading, resistance to that message has continued among many educators and within teacher-training programs.[71] Meanwhile, fluency has often been misinterpreted to simply mean speed, when in fact it refers to reading at a grade-appropriate pace and with appropriate expression. Lack of fluency, which has been called the "bridge" between foundational skills and comprehension, is often the hidden cause of reading difficulties at upper grade levels.[72]

The remaining two elements—vocabulary and comprehension—depend largely on the expansion of children's knowledge. Direct vocabulary instruction is important, especially with regard to words that appear frequently in academic writing, but it can't provide children with all the words they need to become competent readers. The vast majority of working vocabulary comes from repeated exposure to new words in print or spoken language, not explicit word study or memorization. "Almost all the word meanings that we know are acquired indirectly by intuitively guessing new meanings as we get the overall gist of what we're hearing or reading," E. D. Hirsch Jr. has observed.[73] Broad general knowledge across subjects provides the "gist" to which Hirsch refers. It's the key to vocabulary growth and language proficiency, and is particularly critical for disadvantaged children and English learners.

With comprehension, the National Reading Panel discussed only the evidence supporting instruction in certain strategies, omitting any mention of the voluminous evidence that knowledge of the topic is a key factor in comprehension. As a result, many educators wrongly concluded that instructing students in "skills and strategies" was sufficient to build their comprehension.

Alignment to college- and career-ready standards

At their core, college- and career-ready ELA standards require:

- Strong grounding in foundational reading skills (phonics, phonemic awareness, vocabulary, comprehension, and fluency).
- Exposing all students to increasingly complex texts.
- Close reading of these complex texts.
- Reading more informational texts.
- Building background knowledge by reading broadly and diving more deeply into content.
- Organizing units by topic rather than comprehension skill to foster growth in academic knowledge and vocabulary.
- Growing academic vocabulary and syntax.
- Speaking and writing grounded in evidence from texts.

While there are curricula specifically developed with these elements in mind, a 2019 report by the nonprofit organization EdReports estimated that only 16% of school districts are using such ELA curricula in their elementary schools.[74] A 2020 report by the RAND Corporation investigated ELA curriculum, instruction, and standards alignment in three states and found a broad lack of coherence, particularly in elementary school classrooms.[75]

Research demonstrates the imperative for building students' background knowledge and vocabulary. As Susan Pimentel writes, "When students know something about a topic, they are better able to read a text in which that topic is discussed, even when the sentence structure is complex or the words are unfamiliar."[76] Elementary schools' ELA curricula should work to systematically build knowledge and vocabulary across a wide variety of high-interest, culturally relevant texts, including those about history, geography, science, the arts, and more.

At lower grade levels, as students practice and build early reading skills and vocabulary, whether they know something about the topics in their ELA assignments can accelerate or slow their development. Children tasked with unfamiliar topics may experience early failure and learn to dislike reading, leading them to practice less and develop more slowly than their peers. This can exacerbate the "Matthew Effect," the name used by cognitive scientist Keith Stanovich to describe the phenomenon in which the rich get richer and the poor get poorer in vocabulary and knowledge.[77] This hazard looms even larger now, given the massive learning loss experienced by so many students living in poverty.

Expanding access to challenging material

For too long, struggling students were disadvantaged by being provided with lower-complexity texts. The common practice of assigning struggling readers to "just right" texts limits their exposure to grade-level content. Every student, including those with gaps in background knowledge or decoding skills, should be engaged with the curriculum's rich, grade-level texts with appropriate scaffolding and support to address their unfinished learning.[78]

Given the disruptions of the last year, some teachers will have the instinct to provide less complex texts to their students, especially those who appear to have fallen farthest behind. Instead, we must provide these students with more opportunities to grapple with rich and worthy texts and tasks, including those that are culturally relevant and reflective of the students' diversity. And we must provide more support to ensure that students can engage with these texts and achieve year-end goals.

A commitment to these principles will not only build the knowledge and vocabulary so vital to literacy success, but also will fuel engagement and communicate the high expectations we have for all students. And it will begin to inculcate the growth mindset and student agency that characterizes excellent elementary schools.

Providing all students with access to the same knowledge also promotes social and emotional wellbeing. It enables children who would otherwise be relegated to lower-level reading groups to contribute their insights to discussions, demonstrate their capabilities to their peers, and feel that they are full members of the classroom community.

Identifying comprehensive, high-quality curriculum

When making a curriculum selection, a key priority should be on the comprehensiveness of the instructional materials. This suggests:

- There is a distinct strand of the curriculum focused on explicit and systematic instruction in foundational reading skills. Securing solid foundational reading skills early on in students' school careers (ideally by grade 3) allows students to continually develop as fluent readers in every grade level thereafter.

- The curriculum expands the vocabulary children bring to the classroom. It valorizes both text complexity, predominantly through read-alouds in the primary grades, and volume of reading, such as through extended independent reading time, to build knowledge and vocabulary.

- There is coherence in the presentation of topics in order to grow content knowledge. Units are organized by topic, and topics are explored deeply and build on one another sequentially over the school year and across grades. Reading and writing are integrated into science, social studies, music, and other content areas, rather than presented as atomized, skills-based activities. By expanding knowledge of the familiar and broader world, students can develop a trove of knowledge to reference whenever they read.

- Regular, close reading of ever-richer, more complex texts, with supports as needed for universal access and success, expand student understanding. In particular, activities teach students to use evidence when speaking and writing about what the text is communicating.

- The curriculum includes both student- and teacher-facing materials. On-the-spot assessments and end-of-unit performance assessments are part of the curriculum and grounded in its content.

Putting a comprehensive curriculum to its best use in 2021–22 will pose particular challenges after the schooling interruptions in 2020 and the first part of 2021. There are several key questions leaders should consider. How should schools move forward if not all modules were taught in the previous year? Could practices like curriculum compacting (pulling from research on gifted education practices) be employed? How should teachers ensure that the most critical content for each grade level is focused on?

We also should consider other structural changes that leaders and teachers may need to implement. Will second graders who missed out on a great deal of phonics instruction in first grade need more time to work on decoding? Are there elements of the kindergarten curriculum that are typically considered precursors to "kindergarten readiness" that actually must be addressed explicitly? Teachers and leaders will benefit from more specific guidance and support.

Example: EL Education

EdReports has identified a handful of comprehensive, high-quality, knowledge-building, standards-aligned ELA curricula, including several from nonprofit publishers (such as Core Knowledge Language Arts and Wit and Wisdom). We are particularly enthusiastic about EL English Language Arts (EL ELA), which was found to be effective in a 2013 study by Mathematica Policy Research.[79]

We note that this curriculum can be challenging to implement well unless a district has specific, ongoing professional learning supports for teachers and leaders that cover the science of learning and program's overall approach, as well as detailed training on how to use each individual structure within it (see *1.3 – Professional learning* for more).

We hold EL ELA in high regard for the following reasons:

- Its structure builds domain-specific vocabulary and Tier 2 academic vocabulary as well. Each grade is organized into four modules lasting eight weeks, organized around topics like water conservation, ratifying the Nineteenth Amendment, or athletes leading social change. These topics are highly appealing and use rich and engaging texts. Each module contains three units that focus first on knowledge building, then on reading, and then on writing.

- A separate "Skills Block" provides a complete foundational skills program using decodable texts and an aligned suite of assessments.

- It is specifically developed to support social-emotional learning and to meet the needs of English learners.

- It is free and open source. While there are materials costs in implementation, including purchasing the trade books it uses, the curriculum can be accessed free of charge through many different online platforms, including EL Education, Open Up Resources, LearnZillion, and modEL Detroit, which provides school users with lots of flexibility.

- The curriculum is highly educative. It explains pedagogical decisions throughout the materials and includes strong teacher training content through a resource called "your curriculum companion." Topics range from "What makes a text worthy and compelling?" to "How will the curriculum empower my students to own their learning?"

- In 2020, EL Education entered into a partnership with CenterPoint Education Solutions to develop web-based, curriculum-aligned, K–8 interim assessments to mirror the curriculum's scope and sequence and complement the existing formative assessments embedded in the curriculum.[80] This allows teachers to clearly see what concepts students have mastered and which concepts require additional instruction or student practice.

2.3 – WRITING

High-quality elementary school writing curriculum teaches explicit skills through activities that align with the cognitive loads of young students, using content-rich prompts that boost academic learning in all subjects.

Explicit writing instruction not only improves students' writing skills but also helps build and deepen their content knowledge, boosts reading comprehension and oral language ability, and fosters habits of critical and analytical thinking. The process of planning, writing, and revising can be taught in intentional, sequential steps. In following this process, students can improve their skills and overall comprehension and retention of information. It's imperative that schools not scrimp on writing instruction as they help students recover from the pandemic.

To be effective, writing should be embedded in the content of the core curriculum and begin at the sentence level. As Judith Hochman and Natalie Wexler describe in *The Writing Revolution: A Guide to Advancing Thinking Through Writing in All Subjects and Grades*, "Writing and content knowledge are intimately related. You can't write well about something you don't know well. The more students know about a topic before they begin to write, the better they'll be able to write about it. At the same time, the process of writing will deepen their understanding of a topic and help cement that understanding in their memory."[81] They go on to establish six key principles of the Hochman method, which include explicit skills instruction, the infusion of grammar in practice, and an emphasis on planning and revising. These form a strong basis for high-quality, effective writing instruction for all students.

Recommendations

- Adopt and implement a high-quality English language arts curriculum (see *2.2 – Reading*).
- Select a writing curriculum and activities that feature explicit, carefully focused instruction and connect to content across the curriculum,

including by building writing time into all subjects. To date, *The Writing Revolution* (also known as the Hochman method) is the only curriculum that combines these two elements.

- Writing activities should start at the sentence level. Tasking young students with longer assignments will overtax them and short-circuit learning. Sentences are the building blocks for all writing.

- Expand teachers' awareness and enthusiasm for the role that frequent sentence-level writing, sentence expansion and combining, and even note-taking activities can play in enhancing any kind of instruction. A school-wide study of Hochman and Wexler's *The Writing Revolution* can serve as a sound starting point.

- Invest in ongoing curriculum-based professional learning for leaders, instructional coaches, and teachers to build expertise and fully leverage the power of high-quality writing instruction.

Rationale

Content and cognitive science

There is a robust body of research indicating that writing has the potential to boost comprehension and retention, extending back to the 1970s.

In a landmark study, undergraduates were given five minutes to read an article.[82] They then were randomly assigned to one of four tasks: reading the article once; studying it for 15 additional minutes; creating a "concept map" or bubble diagram of the ideas in the article; or writing what they could remember from the passage, known as "retrieval practice." When tested a week later, the group that had engaged in writing had a clear advantage in recalling information and making inferences.[83]

Writing about a topic is akin to preparing to teach something you have learned. Both have been shown to improve recall, a phenomenon called the "protégé effect."[84] Essentially, writing requires students to recall something they have slightly forgotten (the mechanism at work in retrieval practice) and explain it in their own words (the mechanism at work in the protégé effect). This is part of a larger body of research into the impact of "elaborate rehearsal" on memory, which finds that drawing on existing knowledge and actively linking that to new information or ideas, such as by taking notes that restate content in a student's own words, boosts retention.[85] A recent meta-analysis has found that writing about content in science, social studies, and math reliably enhances learning in all three subjects.[86]

And writing can serve as a gateway to student independence and agency. Reading and listening often position students as consumers, but writing and speaking position students as producers of argument, opinion, and ideas.

Most existing approaches to writing instruction fail to take full advantage of these potential benefits. Instead, they ask students to write about their own experiences or about random topics, without providing much background information.

In addition, most instructional approaches vastly underestimate how difficult it is to learn to write. Research shows that writing imposes a heavier cognitive load on working memory than reading.[87] Young students may be juggling everything from letter formation and spelling to putting their thoughts in a logical order. Yet virtually all strategies expect inexperienced writers, including kindergartners, to write multiple-paragraph essays. The theory is that students need to develop their voice, fluency, and writing stamina from the earliest stages. But writing at length only increases cognitive load, potentially overwhelming working memory and depriving students of the cognitive capacity to absorb and analyze the information they're writing about, much less acquire target skills.

The Institute of Education Science's practice guide on elementary writing cites 25 studies finding a variety of positive effects that follow from paying close attention to the writing process.[88] It also recommends that one hour a day be devoted to students' writing beginning in the first grade, and acknowledges that this is unlikely to be achieved unless writing practice occurs in the context of non-ELA content area instruction.

Starting at the sentence level

Studies have shown the positive effects of interventions such as sentence combining and sentence expansion and teaching sentence-construction skills generally, including on students' content knowledge.[89] The IES practice guide recommends that students be taught to construct sentences. There are also indications in the literature on "writing to learn" that shorter writing assignments, including poems, yield larger benefits. In addition, focusing on learning to construct sentences before moving on to paragraphs lightens the load on students' working memory, freeing up cognitive space for absorbing and analyzing the content they're writing about.

And yet for some reason, there appear to be no studies testing whether there are greater benefits from an approach that explicitly teaches students to write sentences *before* asking them to embark on lengthier writing has greater benefits. We hope that such studies will soon be undertaken.

In the meantime, it's best to begin writing at the sentence level. Sentence-level instruction not only lightens cognitive load, it also makes instruction in the conventions of written language—such as grammar and punctuation—far more manageable. Teachers confronted with page after page of error-filled writing often don't know where to begin, and they don't want to discourage students by handing back a sea of red ink. And if students can't write a good sentence, they'll never be able to write a good paragraph or a good essay.

Many students don't easily absorb the mechanics of constructing sentences from their reading, as most approaches to writing instruction assume. Rather, they need to practice how to use conjunctions, appositives, transition words, and so forth. Activities that teach these skills, when embedded in the content of the curriculum, simultaneously build writing skills, content knowledge, and analytical abilities.

For example, students learning about the Civil War might be given the sentence stem "Abraham Lincoln was a great president" and then asked to finish it in three different ways, using "because," "but," and "so." This kind of explicit instruction can also familiarize students with the syntax and vocabulary that are found in written but not spoken language, and can boost reading comprehension. Once you have learned to use a word like "despite" or a construction like the passive voice in your own writing, you're in a much better position to understand it when you encounter it while reading.

Example: The Writing Revolution
The potential of explicit writing instruction that is embedded in the content of the curriculum and begins with sentence-level strategies is enormous. As far as can be determined, the Writing Revolution method is currently the only approach to writing instruction that combines these two features. It rests on six key principles:

- Students need explicit instruction in writing, beginning in the early elementary grades.
- Sentences are the building blocks of all writing.
- When embedded in the content of the curriculum, writing instruction is a powerful teaching tool.
- The content of the curriculum drives the rigor of the writing activities.
- Grammar is best taught in the context of student writing.
- The two most important phases of the writing process are planning and revising.

Once students are ready for lengthier pieces, the Writing Revolution focuses considerable attention on teaching students to construct clear, linear outlines. When students transform their outlines into finished pieces of writing, they are able to construct coherent, fluent paragraphs and essays by drawing on the sentence-level strategies they have been taught. This approach shows students that you can't really separate mechanics from process—or that if you try to, you won't get good results.

2.4 – MATHEMATICS

High-quality elementary math curriculum concentrates on arithmetic while also empowering students to develop mathematical reasoning, discourse skills, and an identity as a learner within a mathematical community.

Remote learning was particularly challenging for students in mathematics. Schools will need to ensure that their "recovery" strategies allow ample opportunities for students to complete unfinished learning before moving on to new concepts.

Adopting and faithfully implementing a high-quality elementary mathematics curriculum that is aligned to college- and career-ready standards—the same curriculum across all grade levels—is one essential step. Such a curriculum does the following:

- Concentrates heavily on arithmetic. Students analyze and solve word problems, practice calculating fluently with mental math and written algorithms, and use the four basic operations on whole numbers, fractions, and decimals.
- Provides sufficient practice with procedures and basic math facts—all developed on a basis of concepts and understanding.
- Enables teachers to orchestrate effective forms of mathematical discourse during lessons, such as eliciting connections between different representations of a problem, or connections between different student strategies.
- Includes effective supports for English learners.
- Enables teachers to involve parents in their children's mathematical education.

Recommendations

- Adopt and implement a single, high-quality elementary mathematics curriculum across all grades and schools that is aligned to college- and career-ready standards. EdReports has given strong favorable reviews to several products, including two we consider exemplars: Eureka Math and

Zearn. Most of their materials are free or low-cost, and both have been adopted widely by some of the best-performing elementary schools in the country.

- Use the same curriculum for interventions and supports—including high-dosage tutoring—that is used for regular classroom instruction.

- Dedicate training and planning time to help teachers develop expertise in the curriculum, including building on what students already know to connect them to grade-level work. In math professional-learning sessions, as in other areas of the curriculum, staff developers should explicitly link what teachers are learning to the curriculum they are using.

Rationale

The research base identifying what works in mathematics education is substantial—probably more so than that of any other subject save for early reading. There are, for example, four different Institute for Educational Sciences practice guides that contain a total of 28 recommendations, all of which are backed by an extensive body of high-quality research.

Most recently, the organization published practice guide 26, *Assisting Students Struggling with Mathematics: Intervention in the Elementary Grades.*[90] It provides six evidence-based strategies and recommendations on how teachers can use them with students with low math achievement: systematic instruction, mathematical language, concrete representations of concepts, number lines, word problems, and timed activities.

In considering the needs of all students, we point to these three recommendations, from IES practice guide 16, *Improving Mathematical Problem Solving in Grades 4 Through 8:*[91]

- Students become more efficient and flexible in selecting appropriate ways to solve problems when they have been regularly exposed to questions that require different strategies to answer. For example, in Eureka Math and Zearn, teachers facilitate classroom discussions about the strategies selected, with questions such as "Which strategy do you prefer and why?" or "Which strategy is the most efficient?"

- Learning to use visual representations is critically important. Students who learn to visually represent the mathematical information in problems prior to writing an equation are more effective at problem solving. High-quality curricula build this progression into the development of all concepts.

- How fractions are treated, beginning in the earliest grades, is a hallmark of high-quality programs. IES reviews the research and concludes that "a high percentage of US students lack conceptual understanding of fractions, even after studying fractions for several years." This conclusion supports using a curriculum that places a high premium on building a conceptual understanding of fractions and the ability to use them to think mathematically.

We also note here the value of faithfully implementing a single math curriculum across an entire school, so students and teachers work with it as designed from grade to grade. When teachers adapt a lesson—arising from good intentions—it can easily vaporize the rigor of a curriculum or defeat its design in other ways. Here are three passages from the 2012 book *Inequality for All*, in which William Schmidt and Curtis McKnight compare instruction among 500 classrooms in six US school districts.[92] They find the greatest variation is not among schools but among individual teachers and illustrate how this contributes to unequal opportunities to learn.

1. "... at the elementary grades, most of the variation among classrooms ... was due to differences in how individual teachers allocated their instructional time across topics—a regrettable outcome, since at these grades teachers are typically not well prepared in mathematics ... More district or school guidance is badly needed to help these teachers, but it is generally not provided."

2. "The vast majority of differences in instructional time for arithmetic at fifth grade were due to differences from teacher to teacher. The large amount of variance in instructional time for arithmetic at the early grades is particularly problematic because instructional time allocated in these early grades lays the foundation for work in later grades. ... differences in content coverage related to number can only foster inequalities that are not only likely to grow in magnitude over time but which could be difficult to eliminate in the subsequent grades, even under the best of conditions. The decisions of individual teachers clearly dominate how time is allocated to instruction in the early grades, and as a result, the variation in those choices is a major source of ... large inequalities..."

3. "In one first-grade classroom, the children spent around six months on place value and whole-number operations (mostly addition and subtraction). The corresponding time was only around one month in another first-grade classroom. ... these are not even the most extreme values in the study, since we have eliminated the 10 percent most outlying values."

Schools also can support students' math development outside of school by engaging families to connect math content to everyday life. For example, the Institute for Education Sciences recently published an activity guide for families of students in grades 2–4, which cues adults to link sharing cookies with learning about fractions.[93]

2.5 – SCIENCE AND SOCIAL STUDIES

High-quality history, geography, and science curricula, taught daily, sequentially impart the knowledge students need to become engaged and informed citizens and are an essential component of literacy achievement.

Science and social studies, including history and geography, are each important in their own right given schools' essential mission to prepare students for citizenship in our democracy. And the critical role that content knowledge plays in learning to read and write is clearly established and has received increased attention in recent years (see *2.2 – Reading* and *2.3 – Writing* for more).

The cultivation of such knowledge will not happen by accident, but instead is the result of systematic exposure to high-quality, content-rich instruction. The use of an outstanding curriculum, taught with care and seriousness, is vital to this pursuit. Elementary schools must protect instructional time for these subjects, including when recovering from pandemic-related learning loss. Schools should commit to 45 minutes each of daily lessons for science and for social studies, but research has shown they typically spend far less time than that on these subjects.[94]

Recommendations

- Establish science and social studies as part of the daily core of elementary school instruction, rather than "special" subjects that happen once or twice a week. Elementary schools should firmly establish knowledge development in history, geography, and science as part of daily practice.
- Adopt and faithfully implement a high-quality science curriculum that is rich in content knowledge and well respected by external reviewers. One curriculum to consider is Amplify Science, the only curriculum with an all-green rating for "coherence and scope" from EdReports.[95] It also received a Tier I "exemplifies quality" rating from Louisiana Believes.[96]
- Adopt and faithfully implement a high-quality social studies curriculum that is rich in content knowledge and culturally relevant. Leading reviewers do not currently rate such programs. Still, we are enthusiastic

about Core Knowledge History and Geography, which provides a comprehensive and sequential exploration of world and American history and geography. It follows the tradition of Core Knowledge's popular ELA curriculum, which earned a Tier I rating from Louisiana Believes and an all-green rating from EdReports.[97]

• Incorporate literacy practices, specifically around fluency and writing, into science and social studies instruction as a lever to improve student outcomes in reading. Building science and social studies knowledge alongside strong literacy practices will lift up a struggling student, almost acting like an intervention. Yet most schools, systems, and teachers do not already see it as such.

Rationale

Learning about science and social studies, especially history and geography, is valuable on its own, and a broad knowledge base in these subjects prepares students to knowledgeably participate in civic life. It also expands their capacity to assimilate new, more complex information related to these areas throughout their schooling and beyond.

Yet too often, elementary schools spend the bulk of instructional time on skills practice that is not grounded in rich content.[98] The cost of a knowledge-light elementary school experience is paid most heavily by children who grow up in poverty. These are the students who often aren't benefiting from summer vacations to Old Faithful in Yellowstone National Park or family conversations over the dinner table about deforestation in the Brazilian rainforest.

This has broad implications for literacy, too. Studies show that when low-income children are explicitly taught the background knowledge contained on tests of reading comprehension, they perform equally as well as their higher-income peers. When reading, students can handle a few unfamiliar words and concepts, but the cognitive load of encountering a wholly unfamiliar subject shuts them down. We know from cognitive science that working or short-term memory stores only a small amount of information. The information stored in a student's long-term memory about a given topic is decisive for their comprehension of new material about the same subject. (For more on this, see *3.1 – Instructional strategies.*)

Consider the "baseball study."[99] Researchers compared the reading comprehension of four groups of students tasked with reading a passage about baseball: "good" and "poor" readers (based on standardized test scores) who either knew or didn't know something about the game. Not only did the poor readers who knew something about baseball outperform the ostensibly good readers who knew nothing, the poor readers who knew something about baseball performed almost as well as the *good* readers who did. This suggests that prior knowledge of the topic of a reading passage compensates for a relative lack of reading "skill."

This has strong implications for social and emotional development as well, particularly for struggling readers. We'd imagine that students with prior content knowledge were far more likely to be engaged and confident in their abilities to read, understand, and contribute to a content-based discussion—all of which contribute to the positive mindset that supports all learning (see *2.6 – Social and emotional learning* for more). This stands in stark contrast to the experience of practicing comprehension "skills" on leveled books. If they do not feel successful in completing less-engaging remedial work, they may come to believe that they are "bad at school." On the other hand, if students are given engaging, rich content that they can access due to their prior knowledge, and are able to grapple with and think deeply about that challenging text, it's likely to have a powerful positive impact on their development and self-image.

International education comparisons find that high-performing countries tend to use high-quality curricula that build content knowledge. A recent study by the Thomas B. Fordham Institute also found that increasing instructional time in social studies is associated with improved reading ability, while more time in English language arts instruction is not.[100] The benefits are particularly strong for girls and children from lower-income or non-English-speaking families.

Good instruction in science and social studies is dependent on curricula that build students' knowledge carefully and systematically. But many school districts rely on teachers without subject-area expertise, or have teachers create their own curricula or piece together lessons from websites like teacherspayteachers.com. In science, this means that students learn random tidbits of knowledge over their elementary school education—frogs one year, butterflies the next, the solar system the following year, and maybe frogs and butterflies again. The lessons might be engaging and interactive, but they lack conceptual integrity. Students rarely gain sufficient prerequisite knowledge to explore new topics in depth, and therefore lack a cohesive understanding of important scientific and historical phenomena.

There's also the longstanding and baseless assumption that history is a developmentally inappropriate topic for children below fourth or fifth grade, and that students' primary interest will be in themselves and their own immediate experience. This is a function of misconceptions about "developmental stages" and "developmental appropriateness" for K–3 students, which have often influenced choices about what to teach in the early grades in these subject areas.[101] The standard elementary school social studies sequence follows a series of "expanding environments" that reflect this assumption: all about me, my family, my neighborhood or community, and so on. Alternatively, some social studies curricula take such a broad approach to "themes" that they become insipid and meaningless.

Both approaches deprive children of the opportunity to expand their knowledge of the world and the vocabulary that goes with it. High-quality programs like Core Knowledge History and Geography avoid these common problems.

2.6 – SOCIAL AND EMOTIONAL LEARNING

Social and emotional learning, or SEL, refers to the skills, values, and attitudes that promote success. As described by CASEL, it is "the process through which children and adults understand and manage emotions, set and achieve positive goals, feel and show empathy for others, establish and maintain positive relationships, and make responsible decisions."

The development of children's social and emotional skills is a longstanding component of elementary education, and may be more important now than ever. Many students will have spent more than a year away from school with limited opportunities to socialize with other children. And some will have experienced significant traumas related to the pandemic, economic downturn, George Floyd's murder, and more.

Effective social and emotional learning (SEL) is best encountered not in standalone programs, but within the context of academic lessons and a broader school culture and climate that provides students opportunities to encounter, reflect on, and practice habits of character. There are several examples of leading definitions and frameworks for SEL development, including those from CASEL (the Collaborative for Academic, Social, and Emotional Learning), the Yale Center for Emotional Intelligence, and Responsive Classroom. These frameworks and activities can be inclusive and recognize and affirm students' diverse cultures when they are integrated into school culture and classroom practice.[102] The proliferation of SEL programs is based on the recognition that students' emotions and social contexts are deeply intertwined with their success in school and beyond, including in the labor market.

Recommendations

- Build SEL into core academic programs, such as English Language Arts, by adopting a curriculum that incorporates the comprehensive teaching of social and emotional skills. For example, the Aspects and Habits of Character promoted in EL Education's English Language Arts curriculum are ready complements to a familiar, widely used definition of SEL.

- Create a school culture, school-wide expectations around student behavior, and expectations for teachers and other staff that focus on supporting and modeling positive social and emotional skills.

By systematically and opportunistically integrating character development into their ELA curriculum, schools can address social and emotional learning far more effectively than only with a standalone program.

Rationale

Supporting students in social and emotional learning can have broad, positive impacts on a host of outcomes. In a 2011 meta-analysis in *Child Development*, the authors analyzed studies of 213 SEL interventions involving more than 270,000 children of varying grade levels.[103] Despite significant variation in the nature of the interventions considered, overall the programs significantly improved students' behavior and academic skills. When they revisited the topic in 2017, the authors confirmed the follow-up effects of SEL interventions on positive academic and behavioral outcomes. (Granted, most of these programs likely were of the standalone type.) In addition, a recent study of Chicago high schools found students had fewer absences, higher grades, and higher rates of graduation when their high schools were better at fostering emotional wellbeing and the habit of working hard.[104] And research also has shown the teachers vary considerably in their ability to teach noncognitive skills with impacts on student achievement, SEL competencies, and behavior and other non-academic outcomes.[105]

While there is not standalone research on the efficacy of the SEL components of ELA programs like the EL curriculum, its SEL features are aligned to those of other strong SEL programs. Specifically, the Aspects of Character integrated into each EL lesson address the features of all strong SEL interventions that demonstrate the highest impact—that they are recurrent, encourage prosocial behavior, and support students' mental health.

Those aspects and habits fall into three core areas: work to become effective learners, work to become ethical people, and work to contribute to a better world. For example, in a third-grade unit titled "Overcoming Learning Challenges Near and Far," students read *Nasreen's Secret School: A True Story from Afghanistan* by Jeanette Winter.[106] While a typical ELA curriculum would likely have used the text to advance students' reading comprehension or analysis skills, the EL curriculum has students discuss and write about questions of democratic values and "standing up for what is right" in the context of a girl forced to attend school secretly.

In addition, although it's an emerging topic of research, there is evidence that SEL programs have a positive impact on the inculcation of democratic values. A 2017 study examined the voting frequency of adults who developed psychosocial skills early on in elementary school.[107] Over 20 years, the study found that students who possessed such skills were more likely to vote as adults.

CHAPTER THREE
INSTRUCTION

3.1 – INSTRUCTIONAL STRATEGIES

Instructional strategies are the techniques and materials teachers use to accelerate student progress, informed by the science of learning.

Some of the most compelling literature on what works in K–12 education comes from cognitive science, which describes how the brain takes in, stores, and retrieves information. The research points to four key instructional strategies that can be used across curricula to maximize learning and the retention of knowledge, stimulate knowledge transfer to related topics, and create opportunities for retrieval and application. They include encouraging active recall, scheduling distributed practice (or spacing), mixing topics together during lessons (or interleaving), and providing frequent feedback.

Recommendations

- Select instructional materials, in part, based on how well they take advantage of the findings of cognitive science.

- Make sure all end-of-unit assessments are cumulative and contain content from previous units. Ideally these assessments will be included in the high-quality curriculum the school adopts.

- Provide teachers with ongoing training in the science of learning, such as by having them read *Make It Stick: The Science of Successful Learning* or participating in The Learning Agency's online course *Learn Better: The New Science of Learning to Learn*.

- Provide teachers with professional development on spacing, interleaving, and retrieval (see below for detailed explanations of these terms).

- Make sure that teacher observation rubrics cue evaluators to look for these instructional practices.

Rationale

High-impact instructional practices rooted in cognitive science mix content topics and vary student activities.[108] They revisit topics over time and challenge students just enough to accelerate development. They draw on different capacities and senses and engage students with aligned assessments and feedback. Here are the key practices and terms:

Encouraging active recall (aka, "retrieval"): One of the most exciting discoveries from learning science is that it appears that the greater the cognitive effort required to retrieve something from memory, the stronger the retention of that information. Lessons should be "just right" in terms of cognitive effort and include plenty of opportunities to recall and use new knowledge and skills.

The evidence also shows that quizzing students is one of the most potent retrieval practices. As explained in the Institute for Education Sciences practice guide *Organizing Instruction and Study to Improve Student Learning*, "The act of recalling information from memory helps to cement the information to memory and thereby reduces forgetting. By answering the questions on a quiz, the student is practicing the act of recalling specific information from memory."[109]

Research also shows that taking a test is "almost always" more effective than spending more time studying the same material, and that students who are tested frequently rate their classes more favorably. Writing, including responding to a writing prompt, can be a powerful retrieval strategy as well.

Scheduling distributed practice (aka, "spacing"): This refers to how teachers time their lessons and assessments. Rather than stacking lessons on the same topic one after the other, delaying re-exposure to material over a period of several weeks and months—whether through homework assignments, in-class reviews, quizzes, or other activities—significantly increases the amount of information students remember.

Mixing topics together during lessons (aka, "interleaving"): This happens when lessons mix content and activities which forces students to shift cognitive gears. Such "varied practice" boosts long-term retention, particularly in math.[110] Rather than studying math operations of a certain type in isolation, for example, it is more effective to mix different topics and types of problems.[111]

Providing feedback to students: In *Make It Stick*, Brown, Roediger, and McDaniel write, "Studies show that giving feedback [on wrong answers to test questions] strengthens retention more than testing alone does and, interestingly, some evidence shows that delaying the feedback briefly produces better long-term learning than immediate feedback."[112] The reason, they suggest, is that learners can quickly become dependent on being corrected.

How to apply these findings to the classroom? We find practitioner-friendly guidance from education psychology professor Barak Rosenshine, whose influential *Principles of Instruction* report formed the basis of the non-exhaustive list below, which first appeared in AFT's *American Educator* magazine:[113]

- Begin a lesson with a short review of previous learning.
- Present new material in small steps, with student practice after each step.
- Ask a large number of questions and check the responses of all students.
- Provide models.
- Guide student practice.
- Check for student understanding.
- Obtain a high rate of success.
- Provide scaffolds for difficult tasks.
- Require and monitor independent practice.
- Engage students in weekly and monthly review.

3.2 – ASSESSING STUDENT PROGRESS

Assessing student progress refers to the ongoing practice of testing students' abilities to retrieve and apply new information and skills, through curriculum-aligned tests, quizzes, and checks for understanding.

Regular curriculum-aligned assessments provide both students and teachers with the feedback they need to improve teaching and learning. Assessments are a means to an end, and should be used to determine *how* to bring students into grade-level instruction, not *whether* to bring them into it.

These can take two major forms. Formative practices, or on-the-spot "dipstick" assessments during lessons such as exit tickets, student work, and student discussions, can be followed up on immediately by teachers. Periodic benchmark assessments at the end of a quarter or unit, such as tests or projects, can be analyzed outside the classroom. Both can provide teachers with detailed information about what students do and do not yet know.

For teachers, data on classroom performance provide insights about their instruction's effectiveness and individual student understanding and misconceptions. For students, timely and meaningful feedback regarding mastery and performance can help them chart progress and better achieve learning goals.

Recommendations

- Select a curriculum in part based on the strength of the varied ways it checks for understanding and how other regular formative assessments are handled within it. Look at whether a curriculum supports teachers to closely track student responses during lessons. We point to the work of Dylan Wiliam on how to use embedded assessments to target instruction and accelerate learning.[114]

- At least once a month, dedicate a grade-level professional learning community meeting to analyzing student work and planning instructional strategies in response.

- In English language arts, distinguish carefully between assessments that uncover problems with foundational skills and those that are aimed at evaluating more complex comprehension issues.

- Guide students to review and reflect on their performance on assessments as a means to accelerate learning, including by setting goals, identifying obstacles, and planning for future success.

Rationale

Our recommendations are heavily influenced by a practice guide published by the Institute of Education Sciences in 2009, *Using Student Achievement Data to Support Instructional Decision Making*.[115] IES published the guide despite acknowledging that the research into using assessments to make instructional decisions is not yet conclusive about what works. This indicates the important role of assessments and how desirable it is that we channel them in the most effective ways possible.

Nonetheless, two of the recommendations informed by the IES guide do have some basis in research findings: making data part of an ongoing cycle of continuous instructional improvement, and teaching students to examine their own data and to set, reflect on, and assess learning goals. Both require knowing how to set learning goals that balance what is meaningful with what is realistic. Setting a goal, in and of itself, is a valuable exercise. But setting a goal that would result in a meaningful outcome and require the student to stretch, but does not set them up to fail, can have a more substantial impact on learning.

Using data to drive continuous instructional improvement means that teachers and instructional leadership teams should:

- **Collect and prepare a variety of data about student learning.** Data from curriculum-aligned and curriculum-embedded assessments are the most valuable, such as those from performance tasks, quizzes, or exit tickets. Students' writing, including sentence-level activities, is another important source of data that has too often been overlooked. These data sets should include a measure of vocabulary, the single most important form of background knowledge.[116]

- **Interpret data and develop hypotheses about how to improve student learning.** Such work should happen independently and in teams, and analyses should be done at the classroom and individual student level. Variability in classroom-level data can provide important insights into expectations and content coverage that teachers and leaders will want to address. In particular, student work analysis is a useful way of developing meaningful hypotheses about student understandings, unfinished learning, and misconceptions. Much of the work of this kind of collaborative reflection will happen during grade-level professional learning community time.

- **Distinguish carefully between assessments that uncover problems with foundational skills (such as phonemic awareness or phonics) and those that are aimed at evaluating reading comprehension.** Poor results on reading assessments are usually interpreted to mean that students require more practice in comprehension skills and strategies, when the struggle may well be with phonemic awareness or the conventions of written language. If the problem is actually a decoding issue, remediation should be targeted to that. If it's a comprehension issue, care should be taken to determine whether the problem was a lack of background knowledge, unfamiliar syntax, or something else. This is one of the areas of greatest challenge. In reading, use of data analysis tools often socializes skill-based versus knowledge-based instruction because the easiest way to cut the data is by standard. Unaddressed it may socialize schools to teach reading incorrectly. In analyzing reading data, it is better to assess mastery of passages based on their text complexity and topical area rather than assessing the mastery of questions by standard.

- **Modify instruction to test hypotheses and increase student learning.** Again underlying the importance of working in subject or grade-level teams, many of the strategies the IES panelists advise for potentially modifying instruction (e.g. targeting intervention, ensuring performance expectations are clear and grade-level appropriate, peer observation) point to the importance of collaborative, curriculum-based professional learning.

Assessments can also help students develop metacognition about their learning, which can support them as they improve their own performance, with the following actions by teachers:

- **Explain expectations and assessment criteria.** Teachers should articulate and share explicit learning goals for lessons and assignments, as well as clear scoring rubrics both before and after assignments are complete.

- **Provide feedback to students that is timely, specific, well formatted, and constructive.** The literature is rich on the importance of each of these.

- **Provide tools that help students learn from feedback.** Such tools include templates asking students to list strengths and weaknesses in their responses, worksheets to facilitate reflection, and charts to track progress.

- **Use students' data analyses to guide instructional changes.** Listening to student reflections on their performance relative to established rubrics can provide useful feedback for teachers. Such reflections also help students develop a sense of agency and ownership of their learning— both of which support all learning and success in adulthood.[117]

3.3 – SUPPORTS FOR STUDENTS WITH DISABILITIES

Supports for students with disabilities refer to techniques and learning designs that scaffold instruction so all students can participate in whole-class, grade-level lessons.

Targeted interventions for elementary school students with Individualized Education Plans (IEPs) should not occur at the expense of their also receiving high-quality, grade-level instruction with the remainder of the class. As much as possible, every opportunity should be provided for student supports that scaffold grade-level instruction, particularly in English language arts, where the development of academic vocabulary and the opportunity to advance oral language competency are vital to literacy success.

When students with IEPs are supported in mainstream settings, an extra adult such as a special-education teacher or paraprofessional often joins the classroom. Their role is critical for both the targeted students and entire class in helping classrooms proactively follow a tiered model of instruction. This serves students with IEPs who need intensive support (Tier 3), more easily provides additional small-group instruction for students approaching grade level (Tier 2), and expands opportunities for teachers to annotate and explain during core, whole-class grade-level instruction (Tier 1).

Recommendations

- Keep struggling students together with their general-education classmates as much as possible, even as their specific learning challenges are also being addressed in small-group Tier 2 settings. The actual instruction students receive in lower-performing groups can be inferior to that received by students in higher-performing groups, much like how assigning students leveled reading books can keep them permanently behind their peers. Look to the Multi-Tier System of Supports (MTSS) framework, which considers tiered instruction within the development of the whole child.[118]

- Structure small-group Tier 2 interventions to maximize their positive impact. The literature is clear about the value of small-group intervention for 20 to 30 minutes per day to help students with learning difficulties or unfinished learning (see *4.3 – Implementation* for specifics).

- Focus Tier 2 time on high-impact skills and topics. Explicit, systematic teaching to develop phonemic proficiency and phonic knowledge is vital and should occur alongside instruction in reading fluency, vocabulary word meanings and word-learning strategies, and comprehension strategies. For more on this, see the IES practice guide on reading RTI.[119] Though more of the literature on multi-tiered instruction has occurred in reading, the principles are equally appropriate for students struggling with mathematics.

- Select and use high-quality instructional materials that include robust discussions, guidance, and tools to lead lessons that meet the needs of all learners and build teachers' capacity to ensure those lessons are accessible and attend to learner variability. Building capacity around Universal Design for Learning (UDL) can help teachers understand diverse learner needs and support stronger scaffolding practices, both of which can better connect all students to complex, grade-level material.[120] Tier 2 interventions should be provided using the core curriculum and be additive, augmenting rather than replacing students' participation in grade-level lessons as part of the class. Again, much of the benefits of such curricula are experienced in a whole-class setting.

Rationale

In its practice guides on Response to Intervention strategies in reading and math, the Institute of Education Sciences cites numerous studies recommending "intensive, systematic instruction in small groups to students who score below the benchmark on universal screening."[121]

In reading, it is recommended that instruction addresses foundational reading skills identified through screening tools and that small groups meet between three and five times a week for 20–40 minutes each time. The science is long on the benefits to students with reading disabilities of extra time spent on explicit, repetitive, structured instruction that can help them make the connections between the sounds of spoken words and the letters that represent those sounds.

In mathematics, the evidence indicates that instruction in these small groups should be explicit and systematic. Lessons should focus on common underlying structures in solving word problems, use visual representations, and build fluent retrieval of basic arithmetic facts.

3.4 – SUPPORTS FOR ENGLISH LEARNERS

Supports for English learners refer to the techniques, strategies, and materials that help students develop language competence while participating fully in core grade-level lessons.

Meeting the particular needs of the diverse and growing group of English learners (ELs) is a pressing challenge for many schools, districts, and charter-management organizations. Although many general education programs and curricula do not provide all of the specific supports ELs need, pullout programs for most students generally do more harm than good.

Specific English-language instruction is appropriate for students with the lowest levels of proficiency, but emerging and developing learners should primarily participate in mainstream grade-level instruction with targeted supports aimed at building their academic vocabulary and oral and written language. This will be particularly important as schools address ELs' unfinished learning in the wake of the pandemic. We acknowledge that some consent decrees require pullout programs for EL students, however.

Recommendations

- Ensure EL students can participate in whole-class, rigorous instruction through scaffolds, including by grounding activities in academic vocabulary and using a curriculum that includes specific EL supports.

- Provide intensive small-group instruction and regular opportunities to develop written language skills based on students' specific learning needs.
- Engage families and build on students' prior knowledge, including home languages and cultural assets.
- Use federal funding earmarked for ELs to offer extended instructional time over and above the regular school day, such as summer and after-school programs and small-group tutoring.

Rationale

Despite disruptions to in-person schooling, districts and schools must identify and offer targeted supports and accommodations to EL students. An EdResearch for Recovery guide rightly recommends using new digital tools to better serve ELs.[122] These include direct outreach to families, such as through translated text messages, as well as new online professional learning for teachers and paraprofessionals.[123] The Institute of Education Sciences published a webinar in February 2021 with recommendations and tools to extend ELs learning at home, including nine caregiver activity worksheets in English and Spanish.[124]

Perhaps the most widely respected guidance on EL instruction has emerged from a project out of Stanford University called Understanding Language. Co-chaired by scholars Kenji Hakuta and María Santos, Understanding Language has considerably advanced educator knowledge about the importance of rigorous, grade-level instruction for ELs. The initiative has articulated six principles for effective lesson planning and delivery.

- Provide ELs with opportunities to engage in discipline-specific practices that build conceptual understanding and language competence in tandem.
- Leverage students' home languages, cultural assets, and prior knowledge.
- Ensure standards-aligned instruction for ELs is rigorous, grade-level appropriate, and provides deliberate and appropriate scaffolds.
- Account for students' English proficiency levels and prior schooling experiences.
- Foster autonomy by equipping EL students with the strategies necessary to comprehend and use language in a variety of academic settings.
- Employ diagnostic tools and formative assessments to measure students' content knowledge and academic language competence.

In its practice guide on the subject, the Institute for Education Sciences considers evidence from 19 separate high-quality studies.[125] The guide supports small-group interventions for EL students, but also stresses "enhancing the core instructional program" in three of its four recommendations. These are:

- Teach a set of academic vocabulary words intensively across several days using a variety of instructional activities.
- Integrate oral and written English language instruction into content-area teaching.
- Provide regular, structured opportunities to develop written language skills.
- Provide small-group instructional intervention to students struggling with literacy and English language development.

The guide also notes that teachers should find ways to group English learners with their non-English-learner peers, because students in heterogeneous groups are likely to benefit from hearing opinions or oral language expressions from students at different proficiency levels. Other discussions of "what works" underscore the importance of explicit and intense instruction in academic vocabulary and the related need for "engaging students in academic discussions about content." Thankfully, several high-quality English language arts curricula on the market are designed to support teachers in delivering instruction that meets the needs of EL students.

Quality language and literacy instruction occurs throughout the school day and across content areas. All teachers in the building, including history, math, science, and other disciplines, should incorporate these recommendations.

3.5 – SUPPORTS FOR LOW-INCOME GIFTED AND TALENTED STUDENTS

Supports for low-income gifted children include how schools identify, group, instruct, assess, and meet the unique needs of academically talented students from less-resourced families.

Now more than ever, high-ability students from low-income families will need specialized attention and guidance from their parents and teachers. Many less-resourced families have experienced illness or personal and financial instability, and low-income students' schooling may have experienced long interruptions due to a lack of resources at home.

Ensuring all students have access to high-quality educational programs and teachers is paramount, and the strategies we outline here would benefit all students. We look at the specific needs of low-income students because the difference in participation in gifted programs between low-income and more affluent students may continue to grow during and after the pandemic if necessary steps are not taken. For example, many well-off families were able to hire private tutors or create pandemic learning pods for their children—setups that many low-income families are less likely to afford. Bright students from disadvantaged families equally deserve targeted supports aimed at cultivating their talents.

Recommendations

Research-based evidence points to six distinctive strategies that can support and challenge gifted children. The National Association for Gifted Children makes the following recommendations[126] to encourage the growth and development of the whole gifted child, including their intellectual, social, emotional, and physical domains:

- **Acceleration** occurs when students move through traditional curricula at rates faster than typical. Its many forms include grade-skipping, early entrance to kindergarten or college, and subject-based acceleration (such as when a fifth-grade student takes a middle-school math course). Many researchers consider acceleration to be an appropriate educational approach that matches the level and complexity of the curriculum with the readiness and motivation of the student.

- **Curriculum compacting** is a technique for differentiating instruction for students who have already mastered the material to be learned. Rather than cueing students to practice what they already know, teachers replace whole-class content with new content, enrichment options, or other activities. This important instructional strategy condenses, modifies, or streamlines the regular curriculum to reduce repetition, allowing time for acceleration or enrichment.

- **Grouping**, or placing students with similar abilities or performance levels together for instruction, has been shown to improve achievement. Grouping gifted children together allows for more appropriate, rapid, and advanced instruction, to better match their quicker pace of development—and benefits them socially and emotionally.

- **Identification**, or the process by which students are categorized as gifted, is a critical component of effective education for advanced students. Gifted learners exhibit different characteristics, traits, and ways to express their giftedness. It is critical for teachers and school administrators to use assessments and criteria that recognize that giftedness is dynamic, not static, and is represented across all races, ethnicities, and income levels. Different strategies may be needed to ensure diverse students with high potential are identified. One size does not fit all.

- **Pullout and other specialized programs** are among the diverse programming options for gifted and talented students. Research demonstrates the effectiveness of these varied options, such as gifted pullout classes in a subject or standalone schools run by the state (such as the Indiana Academy for Science, Mathematics, and Humanities). Gifted students also benefit from local magnet schools or gifted programs that occur after school, on Saturdays, or during summer.

- **Teacher training** is critical to high-level gifted programs, because teachers who know how gifted students learn can use gifted education strategies in the classroom. Because most gifted children spend their school days in regular classrooms, providing basic training for all teachers on how to recognize and serve advanced students can help them more appropriately educate those pupils.

CHAPTER FOUR
RECOVERING FROM THE PANDEMIC

4.1 – TARGETED HELP AND HIGH-DOSAGE TUTORING

Targeted help and high-dosage tutoring seek to address unfinished learning through acceleration and structured learning supports, not remediation.

A growing body of evidence indicates that many students experienced a substantial amount of unfinished learning during the pandemic. The tendency of educators may be to use benchmark assessments to determine the extent of unfinished learning and then group those students according to how far below grade level they've fallen. While benchmark assessments can be helpful, evidence suggests that grouping struggling students in this manner is not the approach to use because it leads to them spending most of their time doing below-grade-level work.

A consensus is emerging among well-respected organizations with instructional expertise that schools should instead focus on accelerating these students and supporting them to participate in grade-level instruction. Targeted support to help all students reach grade-level goals should be curriculum-specific, and the support itself should focus on the most critical skills and knowledge students need to master by the end of the school year. Researchers and practitioners are focused in particular on the potential of intensive tutoring to address learning losses caused by the Covid pandemic.

Recommendations

- Articulate the most critical instructional content priorities and benchmarks for grade-level success and focus instruction accordingly.

- Maintain grade-level instruction for students with unfinished learning and use regular assessments to deliver just-in-time acceleration, as needed. Teaching at grade level is about keeping up, not catching up, but using frequent formative assessments can identify missing skills or content knowledge so that gaps can be addressed at the right moments.

- Extend the school day to provide high-impact, high-dosage tutoring using proven practices.[127] These include student–tutor ratios no greater than 4:1, instruction that complements classroom lessons, ample time to meet at least three times each week, and sustained relationships between students and well-supported, well-trained tutors.

Rationale

Acceleration

David Steiner of Johns Hopkins University and Dan Weisberg, formerly of TNTP, write that "'meeting students where they are' and trying to remediate learning deficits often just results in having to meet them even further back next year. It stigmatizes students and reinforces inequities. ... Instead of delaying access to grade-level work for students who've fallen behind, we need to accelerate it."[128] A report from TNTP and Zearn finds that students who experience acceleration learn more than those who receive remedial instruction, and that acceleration is especially effective for low-income students of color.[129]

In her book, *Learning in the Fast Lane: 8 Ways to Put ALL Students on the Road to Academic Success*, Suzy Pepper Rollins writes, "Remediation is based on the misconception that for students to learn new information, they must go back and master everything they missed."[130] Rollins goes on to say that while the primary focus of remediation is mastering concepts in the past, acceleration prepares students for success in the present. "Rather than concentrating on a litany of items that students have failed to master, acceleration readies students for new learning. Past concepts and skills are addressed, but always in the purposeful context of future."

In the context of the broad interruptions in schooling due to the pandemic, educators will need to quickly diagnose and offer some remedial support for missing foundational skills. When it comes to reading, however, schools must take care not to rely on assessments, instruction, or remediation that focus primarily on comprehension skills or strategies. Students should not be tested for their individual "reading levels" and then limited to books at those supposed levels. Some young students will likely need to experience a booster shot of explicit instruction in decoding, for example, to ensure they can read and comprehend. However, the key is not to start wholly over, but strategically identify and support skill gaps that hamper future learning—and to ensure students don't lose out on instructional time and access to grade-level content in social studies and science.

A number of well-respected organizations, including Student Achievement Partners, Council of the Great City Schools, Achievement Network, the Center for Assessment, the Center on Reinventing Public Education, and TNTP, have provided guidance related to acceleration to address unfinished learning. In all cases, the advice is in support of grade-level instruction for students.

The Evidence Project, a collaborative research effort led by the Center on Reinventing Public Education "to close the gap between research and policy in K–12 responses to COVID," published a paper with this specific advice: "Focus on what's most important for a student to know to engage effectively in the first major unit or two of the instruction."[131] As a teacher moves forward in the curriculum, experts suggest working in grade-level teams to identify the most critical prerequisite skills and background knowledge students will need to access the upcoming content and address this in "real time," as the unit is being taught.

Student Achievement Partners, whose founders are the lead authors of the Common Core State Standards and other college- and career-ready standards, issued a helpful document in the summer of 2020 that identified the priority instructional content in ELA/literacy and mathematics.[132] Publishers have used this document to support teachers in collapsing content that is not as essential to the major work of the grade and pulling in material from units that students missed previously, as needed.

Scott Marion of the Center for Assessment argues that off-the-shelf assessment products are disconnected from the instruction they intend to measure. A better approach is to select instructional materials that come with aligned assessments baked into them, through both formal assessments and other opportunities throughout the curriculum itself to assess student learning such as exit tickets, written work, or student discussions. As Student Achievement Partners notes, such an approach is a "deliberate alternative to assessment choices that have the potential to serve as a gatekeeper to grade-level content."

The choice of curriculum can help. For example, there is evidence that the kind of writing instruction embodied in the Writing Revolution's method can help compensate for significant gaps in background knowledge and facilitate acceleration. In a high school where many students lacked sufficient preparation for grade-level work, its adoption led to significantly higher graduation rates and

AP participation, as well as improvements in other measures of achievement over a three-year period.[133] If such an approach can compensate for 10 years or more of deficient in-class education, it is likely to help with the negative effects from the much shorter period of remote schooling during the pandemic.

Tutoring

An important programmatic feature of any school's acceleration design must be the strategic use of tutoring.[134] Education researcher Robert Slavin, who was director of the Center on Research and Reform in Education at Johns Hopkins University until his recent death, has argued that intensive tutoring is, by far, the most effective intervention for students who have fallen behind. Given the scope of the challenge, he said, "it would be malpractice to do anything less than tutoring."[135]

The educational benefits to high-dosage tutoring are immense. A meta-analysis of nearly 200 research studies finds that high-dosage tutoring has a far greater effect on math and reading outcomes than even early childhood interventions.[136] Gold-standard randomized experiments have demonstrated the incredible gains students can make with the help of a tutor.[137] For example, in Chicago, at-risk high school boys rose from the 38th percentile to the 46th percentile of math achievement.[138] Furthermore, tutoring is an intervention with the potential to scale well across contexts. In Houston, high-dosage tutoring models successfully transferred from high-performing charter schools to lower-performing traditional public schools.[139]

In addition to significant learning loss, students have spent the past year feeling increasingly disengaged from their school communities.[140] Tutoring has been shown to improve attendance and engagement among students, with results similar to programs like Success Mentors in New York City.[141] As reported by Harvard's Center on the Developing Child, students with at least one positive and stable adult relationship are far more capable of responding successfully to traumatic events.[142] These benefits are present even in a virtual capacity. In Italy, a fully remote tutoring program significantly improved the psychological wellbeing of students in the spring of 2020.[143]

Recommended sources of guidance and expertise

The new National Student Support Accelerator, housed at the Annenberg Institute at Brown University, was launched to accelerate the growth of high-impact tutoring opportunities for K–12 students in need. The accelerator coordinates and synthesizes tutoring research, and uses that research to develop publicly available tools and technical assistance for districts and schools.

The accelerator began with a group of national education leaders seeking solutions to pandemic-disrupted learning. Initial research by the group quickly identified tutoring as a promising solution for three major reasons: its effectiveness relative to other academic interventions, spillover effects such as increased student engagement, and ability to improve the teacher-employment pipeline, by providing opportunities for a large and diverse group of potential teachers to gain direct experience working with students, build their skills, and deepen their understanding of teaching.

However, not all tutoring is effective or equitable. For example, the Supplemental Education Services provision of the No Child Left Behind act inspired a massive investment in tutoring programs at underperforming schools. But less than one-quarter of eligible students participated and evaluations showed little benefit, on average.[144] Guidance published by Ed Reform Now, The Education Trust, and FutureEd shares research, recommendations, and examples from Colorado and Louisiana of high-impact tutoring programs.[145]

The National Student Support Accelerator defines high-impact tutoring as "a form of teaching, one-on-one or in a small group, toward a specific goal" that "leads to substantial learning gains for students by supplementing (but not replacing) students' classroom experiences."[146] Such tutoring "responds to individual needs and complements students' existing curriculum." Importantly, these tutors form meaningful relationships with students and should not serve students on a rotating or drop-in basis.[147]

This model captures several of the characteristics identified as making tutoring more effective in a recent analysis by The Education Trust and MDRC.[148] It also mirrors research-based recommended supports for students with disabilities and echo recommendations published by the Institute for Education Sciences in its practice guides on Response to Intervention in reading and math.[149] Specifically, effective tutoring programs should include:

- A minimum of three sessions of at least 30 minutes per week.
- Sustained, strong relationships between student and tutor.
- Student–tutor ratios no greater than 4:1.
- Close monitoring of student knowledge and skills.
- Alignment with the school curriculum.
- Oversight of tutors to assure quality interactions.

Matthew Kraft and Grace Falken of Brown University recommend that tutoring be made available to every student and incorporated into the school day, including by extending the school day by 30 minutes.[150] By providing a tutor to every student, schools can decrease the stigma around receiving extra help and eliminate the perception of tutoring as a "punishment" for low performance. Incorporating tutoring into a part of the regular school day also promotes "regular attendance, better coordination with teachers, and a stronger academic culture," they write.

Extended learning time has been shown to be a successful strategy for delivering additional needed instruction. For example, targeted instruction provided to select students over school breaks and weekends at turnaround schools in Massachusetts both improved student achievement and lowered suspension rates.[151] But given the urgency and wide-scale need for additional instruction, extending the school day to allow for tutoring is likely to be a far more implementable and sustainable strategy.

Using just-in-time techniques

We are impressed by the advice of the National Council of Teachers of Mathematics as it relates to just-in-time support for students due to pandemic-related school interruptions, and think it has implications for this tutoring strategy as well.[152] The council advises:

> "There are better options than using testing at the beginning of the school year to assess a laundry list of prerequisite understandings from previous grades that would consume a significant amount of instructional time. Prerequisite skills or understandings that may have been missed as a result of COVID-19 could be strategically taught right before the connected unit of study or incorporated as spiral review or as part of instructional routines and procedures. Teaching these skills as connected to grade-level or course-level content deepens students' mathematical understanding.

> "Before each unit of study, teachers should collaboratively identify prerequisite understandings, using sources such as the Mathematics Coherence Map, that will build the foundational understanding for the essential learning in each unit of study students are about to enter.[153] They should collaboratively plan how to support students in making connections to previous learning, incorporating tasks and lessons that build conceptual understanding before the unit of study."

We also point to the Learning Acceleration for All guide from TNTP and Priority Instructional Content guides in reading and math from Student Achievement Partners as useful tools for this process.[154]

Still, not all teachers will feel prepared or as though they have time enough for this separate stage of review. For those teachers, using diagnostic tools or supplementary lessons already built into a high-quality curriculum can inform instruction and tutoring needs, such as EL Education's *Flex* and *Eureka Math Equip* from Great Minds.

Schools and districts can staff tutoring efforts by tapping teacher-preparation programs, paraprofessionals, and trained volunteers. Tutoring should be delivered to students identified by classroom teachers and be closely related to classroom instruction. Tutors might preview upcoming grade-level content or address unfinished learning relevant to upcoming lessons. To ensure tutoring is high quality, schools should focus on the "what" of each session: what content, what tasks, what routines. Tutoring should be simple and focused on accessing core instruction. One example of this approach is the Minnesota Reading Corps program, which trains AmeriCorps members on 11 straightforward, research-based reading routines and has tutored more than 200,000 students to date, according to their website.

Implementation: Decisions to consider

An important caveat is that much of the research on tutoring fails to distinguish between different kinds of tutoring: math, decoding, or reading comprehension skills and strategies. (There has been little or no tutoring in social studies, science, or any other content area, especially at the elementary level.) A recent meta-analysis observed that "curriculum and other pedagogical characteristics of tutoring interventions remain mostly black-boxed in our review."[155] It also found that in reading, the benefits of tutoring are highest at lower grade levels, after which a "pattern of declining returns."[156] On the other hand, math tutoring tends to be more effective in later grades.

Moreover, effectively scaling up tutoring programs is no easy feat. Context and quality matter. For high-dosage tutoring to reach many more students than it currently does, policymakers will have to make well-informed choices and do more than just throw money at these programs.[157] Quality implementation is everything.

We raise the question here of whether reading tutoring should be targeted at lower-level readers rather than just lower-grade readers—consider the middle-school student, for example, with weak decoding skills. The impacts of this sort of tutoring may not be as immediately evident as grade levels go up, possibly because decoding skill becomes less important and background knowledge becomes more important, since more complex texts assume more background knowledge. At any grade level, "reading" tutoring that focuses only on decontextualized comprehension skills should be avoided, since it will only set students up for failure at higher grade levels, just as with regular classroom instruction. But tutoring that specifically targets missing or underdeveloped decoding skills is crucial.

Nothing in this discussion should be confused with a lack of commitment to addressing diagnosed special learning needs with appropriate Tier 2 and Tier 3 instruction (see *3.3 – Supports for students with disabilities* for more). This discussion relates specifically to learning losses attendant to pandemic-related school closures. By extension, however, much of it could also apply to students with learning gaps or unfinished learning due to other circumstances, such as chronic absenteeism, ineffective prior instruction, previously undiagnosed special needs, social-emotional challenges, or lack of exposure to phonics or other essential parts of the curriculum. These challenges are likely to be intersectional, with the most substantial learning losses among students who were already academically behind their peers.

4.2 – EXPANDED MENTAL HEALTH SUPPORTS

Rather than responding in crisis, expanded mental health supports guide and nurture students and staff to process trauma, restore their equilibrium within the school community, and participate fully in teaching and learning.

As schools move to fully reopen, our first inclination may be to focus on the learning gaps that students have developed during the pandemic. But the psychological and emotional wellbeing of all members of a school community must also remain in the foreground. Establishing school as a space that is both physically and emotionally safe is essential (see *the 1.4 – Safe and supportive climate* for more). All students and teachers have experienced unprecedented disruptions to normal patterns of interaction, and many have had to cope with uncertainty or substantial hardship. They will need support as they transition back into a full-time academic environment. In addition, many students will be managing grief, anxiety, or other emotional responses to recent events that will require long-term monitoring and an ongoing response.

Amid the instability of the 2020–21 school year, school leaders identified students' mental health as one of their top concerns. A recent survey of more than 32,000 caregivers found widespread growth in child mental health concerns.[158] However, most educators do not feel confident in their ability to identify students who might require additional mental health supports.[159] Furthermore, many schools lack a clear, coherent system for addressing students' mental health needs. Roughly 40% reported that they currently address concerns on a "case by case basis."

This is not a new challenge. According to the US Department of Health and Human Services, one in five children and adolescents experience a mental health problem during their school years. While some schools have found ways to add the required resources through complicated funding and staffing pictures, others have struggled to get even one mental health professional on campus. With the sudden influx of federal Covid relief funds, the financial barriers to providing these services in schools are disappearing, at least temporarily.

The time for ad hoc responses is over. Having a distinct plan in place as students and educators reacclimate to the classroom environment will be an integral component to ensuring the wellbeing of students.

Recommendations

Our recommendations fall into five major types of action:

- **Hiring**: The simplest and most effective way to provide comprehensive mental health services on campus is for schools to hire mental health professionals on staff. The current recommended ratio is one for every 250 students; however, with the increased needs in the wake of Covid, that may not be enough.

- **Triage**: Perform formal or informal triage to identify what students need to support their learning, and establish a referral system to connect students with school- and community-based mental health resources.

- **Trauma-informed practices**: Expect students to have difficulty with the transition back into classrooms. Establish generalized supports that can benefit all students, specifically trauma-informed relational practices and a robust framework for social and emotional learning that promotes emotional wellbeing and social connectedness.

- **Targeted intervention**: Monitor for behaviors that indicate a need for targeted intervention. Support school-based mental health professionals in implementing an evidence-based mental health program, such as Cognitive Behavioral Intervention for Trauma in Schools (CBITS), for students who have experienced significant trauma or who have been diagnosed with serious mood, anxiety, or other behavioral disorders.

- **Faculty support**: Attend to the mental health needs of faculty and staff by providing appropriate resources, developing a culture of emotional openness and vulnerability, building structures to support social engagement, and helping individuals develop their self-care practice.

Rationale

Hiring

School mental health is its own subset of mental health, and not all licensed practitioners are prepared for what it means to be in a school setting. Schools should be clear about the expectations for student services and any limitations they would put in place, such as students not being pulled from core classes. Possible provider types include licensed psychologists, licensed clinical social workers (LCSW), licensed master social workers (LMSW), and licensed professional counselors (LPC).

Adding headcounts can be a tricky proposition for school districts using federal stimulus funds to make new hires. It raises the obvious question: what happens when that temporary support runs out? This is an area where using approved contractors, who can offer specialized supports across multiple schools, may be wise.

In addition, recent changes to federal Medicaid guidelines have opened up a potential pathway for long-term funding of these services.[160] In 2014, Medicaid released updated guidelines known as the Free Care Reversal Policy that clarified that states can allow schools to bill Medicaid for mental health services for all students—not just those with IEPs, which is how Medicaid had previously functioned. This pathway has the potential to provide long-term sustainable funding for schools to provide these mental health services. However, each state must go through a process to authorize this change, and to date, only 13 have.[161]

Triage

As with anything else in a school, in order to know what a student needs, their current ability must be assessed. This is no different in mental health. All schools should have a universal screening tool in place to be completed for all students before or immediately after the beginning of the year.

Keep in mind, however, that these screening tools can do more harm than good if schools do not follow up with services. If educators ask a student what they need and the screening tool shows they need support for depression or anxiety but the school does not then provide that service, the student learns that being vulnerable and asking for mental health support does not mean that that support will come.

We know that students have experienced the pandemic in different ways. While some may not have weathered significant anxiety or personal hardship, others have experienced traumatic personal events. This is most common among low-income students and students from racial and ethnic minorities, whose families are far more likely to have suffered economic hardship, illness, and death.

Students who have been physically separated from their school or community may feel isolated or neglected, including those who are vulnerable in their homes as a result of the volatility or abusive behavior of a family member. Many students, and particularly Black students, may also be contending with anxiety, fear, or confusion in a climate of anti-Black racism and police violence.

Knowing the state of any one student's emotional wellbeing is difficult, unless they voluntarily disclose that information or, perhaps more likely, exhibit stress-induced behaviors like misbehaving (externalizing) or shutting down (internalizing). And educators must be ready to support all students, without treating them all the same. Mary Walsh, a professor of counseling and developmental psychology at Boston College, has estimated that even among students who have experienced trauma during the period of the closure, only about one-third are likely to develop serious issues, such as PTSD.[162] Monitoring students for behavior changes will be important, but Walsh cautions against pathologizing students, suggesting that "If we put the right protective factors in place, kids have enormous resilience."

The American School Counselor Association and the National Association of School Psychologists recommend collecting data to inform a psychological "triage" approach, to allow schools and districts to identify students who need mental health supports most.[163] That includes students who have lost someone close to them, whose families have experienced financial distress or dislocation, who have previous mental health concerns, and who have a history of trauma, including membership in a community with previous history of educational disruption (such as natural disasters or mass casualties).

The next step is to connect students to appropriate services. Selecting those services should not be done on a case-by-case basis. Rather, staff need to have a clear understanding of what is available to best respond to student needs well in advance of any incident. A clear process for referrals can make this step more efficient and maximize the impact of this response.

Project AWARE Ohio has detailed a comprehensive referral protocol to help schools and districts identify gaps in current procedures:[164]

1. **Establish a problem-solving team for referrals.** If there is no pre-existing team with capacity to manage referrals, team members will need to be established and the team's purpose, responsibilities, routines, and evaluation procedures articulated.

2. **Determine a procedure for managing referral flow.** Adopt a standard referral form, determine a process for submission, and communicate this process with the school community. If referrals will be made to community agencies, identify key contacts.

3. **Develop a system for the team to gather student background information.** Establish norms for collecting data from triage screenings, behavioral observations, and interviews with family and school personnel.

4. **Establish a secure record-management system.** Determine where data will be stored and ensure that access is limited to appropriate team members.

5. **Map available resources and interventions.** Create a database of school- and community-based resources and available interventions. Establish community partnerships, when appropriate, to fill gaps and discuss how the referral time will address barriers to access.

6. **Create decision rules to determine appropriate interventions based on this information.** Establish guidelines on how students will be identified for the different tiers of intervention that are available and a plan for evaluating whether interventions are effective or should be discontinued.

7. **Develop a system to monitor and evaluate intervention effectiveness.** The team should establish procedures for tracking whether interventions are occurring, whether they are effective, and how to request and share information and feedback between the involved parties (such as students, families, school personnel, and community partners).

The team at the core of this system should follow a holistic "Student of Concern" (SOC) team structure, to include representatives of the academic, physical health, mental health, behavior, special education and any other unique school aspect needs of students. This team should meet weekly with a set agenda of students to discuss. Each student brought to the attention of the team should be viewed from a holistic perspective and a plan to meet their needs created with concrete follow-up assignments for each team member. Schools can consider using federal Covid funds for a support staff member to ensure this team's goals are met. This team-based approach is also reflected in a recent EdResearch for Recovery brief on addressing trauma and stress among students, which recommends schools avoid placing the burden for supporting students on counseling staff.[165]

Trauma-informed practices

Trauma is a psychological or emotional response to "an event, series of events, or set of circumstances that is experienced by an individual as physically or emotionally harmful or life threatening," according to the federal Substance Abuse and Mental Health Services Administration.[166] Many students and families have personally experienced trauma related to health and economic consequences of the pandemic. And the period of disruption itself may have been traumatic for some. Viewing these events as presenting multiple potential traumas can help guide school policies, practices, and interactions among staff and students.

The adoption of trauma-informed practices in schools has steadily gained steam over the past several years. Dr. Howard Bath, a clinical psychologist and expert in developmental trauma, has identified three key pillars of trauma-informed care: safety, connections, and managing emotional impulses.[167]

Ensuring students feel safe is essential. Even in the absence of a distinct threat, the brains of traumatized children tend to remain in a state of alarm, with energy focused on ensuring safety rather than engaging in growth-promoting activities. Creating consistent, reliable, and predictable environments in which students feel they have a degree of power and choice can help establish school as a safe place where they can relax their guard and trust the adults that they interact with regularly.

Trust and the perception of safety cannot occur without the second pillar, connections. Positive relationships with caring adults have great therapeutic value and may help to counteract negative associations from past experiences. Educators can foster such relationships by attending to, validating, and creating space for the strengths that students bring to the classroom. This also supports students seeing themselves as competent, worthwhile individuals.

Maintaining compassionate connections is complicated, however, by the difficulty traumatized individuals often have in self-regulation and managing emotional impulses. Responses to trauma are frequently observed as behavioral responses. In a school environment, where establishing strong routines and behavioral norms is a necessary part of creating a physically and emotionally safe space, trauma may prevent students from complying with all expectations for behavior right away. Students will need time to adjust, and disobedience may simply be a function of students' challenges to regulate themselves.

Educators need to keep this in mind, rather than categorizing behavior as willful disobedience. Rather than assuming that negative classroom behaviors (such as outbursts, defiance, or shutting down) are intentional and responding in a punitive fashion, trauma-sensitive educators help students "co-regulate" by modeling and explicitly teaching students how to manage their emotional impulses. Connectedness with peers is also an important protective factor, both for students dealing with trauma and those with other mental health conditions. Explicit social and emotional learning instruction can help facilitate these relationships.

While the field of trauma therapy in schools is still developing, EMDR (Eye Movement Desensitization and Reprocessing) therapy is well researched and highly effective at alleviating stress from traumatic memories, according to the EMDR Institute website. Licensed mental health practitioners can be trained in EMDR in a relatively short amount of time. Schools with student populations who have experienced significant levels of trauma should consider using some of the federal Covid relief funds to pay for their mental health practitioners to be trained in EMDR. This is a one-time expense that can have a long-term positive effect for individual schools.

Targeted intervention

A strong mental health program should offer a diverse array of services and be tied into every aspect of the school day. Though adopting trauma-informed practices as generalized supports is beneficial, for some students that won't be sufficient support. A subset of students will have had direct traumatic experiences or be suffering from mental health conditions. They will need intensive interventions above and beyond generalized trauma-informed care in order to be ready to learn.

School leaders cannot assume these students will receive appropriate treatment outside of school, since approximately one-third of all adolescents who receive mental health care are served *only* in the setting of their school.[168] This is particularly true for students who identify as members of a racial or ethnic minority or who come from a low-income household. Responding appropriately to these students' needs will take the involvement of all staff members with mental health training, including school counselors, psychologists, social workers, and nurses.

Tools for coping: Some students were out of a regular classroom for more than a year, and returning to that environment will be an overstimulating experience for many. In addition to mental health staff, schools should have tangible tools to help students cope on campus, such as headphones, music options, and quiet rooms that give them a break from excessively stimulating environments. Students who display more severe symptoms of overstimulation should receive individual plans to help them ease back into the school environment. Schools can use federal Covid funds for plans prepared by a qualified mental health professional.

Group therapy: Well-done groups are one of the most effective therapeutic techniques for schools. They not only help students address common mental health concerns but also facilitate interpersonal social-emotional growth. From an organizational perspective, groups allow one mental health professional to serve multiple students in a shorter amount of time. Schools can explore adding a group session before, after, or during a regular school day to meet student needs for families who opt in.

Potential Covid-related group topics include: grief, for students who have lost family and friends to the pandemic; germaphobia or compulsive tendencies, for students who have internalized hand washing and mask wearing to the extreme; and sensory issues, for students who are struggling to return to large and busy buildings after spending months in the relative quiet of their homes.

Schools with enough specialized staff can offer individual and group-based interventions such as Cognitive Behavior Intervention for Trauma in Schools (CBITS). Multiple studies have demonstrated that students who participate in a CBITS program experience significant improvement in self-reported symptoms of post-traumatic stress compared to a control group.

Suicide prevention: In order to correctly identify students who are at-risk for suicide, schools must do comprehensive training for all staff members (not just teachers) on how to look for risk signs and what to do if they find them. This training should take place during summer professional development, but it should also be an ongoing topic throughout the year. Schools should have a set process to evaluate student risk and a clear plan of what to do if the student is an immediate risk to themself or others (going to the hospital immediately) or is not a current active risk but may be at some point (create a safety plan). A good safety plan should help students and the people around them identify potential triggers for self-harming behavior and have places to go, people to speak to, and emergency numbers to call if a student feels unsafe.

Regardless of the intervention approach, it is important to ensure that administration and instructional staff all have a shared understanding regarding the importance of these interventions. And it is critical to remember that there will always be some students whose needs are too urgent or intensive to be served within the school setting. Intensive interventions should be handled in collaboration with external partners.

Attend to staff needs

No mental healthcare plan would be complete without considering the needs of the adults in the building, especially those in student-facing roles. The past year—full of sleepless nights, radical changes to instruction, long hours, unexpected childcare duties, and worries about safety for their students and themselves—has taken a toll on educators. A Louisiana study found that the prevalence of clinically significant symptoms of depression had almost doubled among early childhood educators.[169] And in another study, approximately 85% of teachers reported that their mental health had declined compared to the previous year.[170]

The recovery period already threatens to be a pressure cooker for teachers. They are burdened with the expectation to make up for months of lost learning while also accommodating students' heightened social and emotional needs. Proactive planning can help educators feel supported in their work and decrease instances of burnout that may lead to ineffective instructional environments or turnover. When referring to "burnout," we adopt the definition used by The World Health Organization: the feelings of exhaustion, negativity, or cynicism, and the reduced professional efficacy that may result from insufficiently managed and/or chronic workplace stress.[171]

Developing an organizational culture in which frank and open conversations can occur about staff emotions and mental health takes time, but schools and districts can nonetheless teach strategies and create structures that lay the groundwork for a healthy and open workplace.

First and foremost, schools should ensure that staff members have appropriate access to mental health care, such as counselors or therapists. Adequate coverage must be available so that staff have the ability to take the time they need to address their healthcare and personal needs. These basic supports can be bolstered by building in intentional opportunities for staff to connect with each other, whether by having periodic "check-ins," developing mentorship relationships, or creating opportunities to socialize or decompress with other adults in the school community. To ensure educators take advantage of these supports, it can be productive for leaders to model emotional vulnerability and help-seeking behaviors. That helps staff to view these practices as indicators of strength rather than weakness.

It is also important to encourage stress-management strategies, such as healthy eating, exercise, adequate sleep, and relaxation techniques, including by weaving them into school culture. In particular, mindfulness practices have been shown to be effective in helping teachers manage occupational stress. There are a variety of models and resources that organizations can adopt depending on their unique circumstances. The Cultivating Awareness and Resilience in Education (CARE) professional development program, which teaches mindfulness techniques, has been shown to improve teacher wellbeing, efficacy, burnout, and stress.[172] Freely available resources such as Diana Tikasz's excellent Pause-Reset-Nourish framework can also be helpful.[173]

Above and beyond these practices, leadership should pay particular attention to staff members who seem to have difficulty coping with the challenges of their role and offer support as needed. Educators working in areas of high poverty or high trauma may be at risk of developing secondary traumatic stress (STS), in which they experience trauma due to hearing about the traumatic experiences of their students. While similar to burnout in terms of its external expression, STS is often not alleviated by a change in occupational environment. Particular educators may be more susceptible, including those who have experienced trauma themselves, are highly empathetic or inexperienced, or who work in communities that have experienced elevated levels of poverty, crime, or tragic events. The organization Support for Teachers Affected by Trauma offers a free training program to help educators recognize symptoms and engage in protective strategies.

As the adage goes, you need to put on your own oxygen mask first before helping others. Once we've done that, we're better equipped to get through this turbulence together.

4.3 – IMPLEMENTATION

Helping students recover from the effects of the Covid pandemic and the other crises of the past year is likely the greatest challenge that most of today's educators will ever face. It will take extensive time, skill, and collaboration between leaders, teachers, staff, and families. And it will look different from community to community—and even from school to school.

Two key questions are how instructional leaders might sequence the implementation of various pieces of a recovery plan, and how to bring them into a coherent whole. This section features our thoughts on that, as well as a model student-and-teacher schedule that shows what all of this might look like in practice.

Recommendations

- **Put the basics in place before adding new elements, especially high-dosage tutoring. Adopting and helping teachers implement a high-quality curriculum is job No. 1.** Many elementary students, especially those in high-poverty schools, will need extra help to recover from the loss of instructional time related to the pandemic. Done right, high-dosage tutoring shows great promise in helping such students return to grade level. But doing it right means integrating tutoring with regular classroom and small-group instruction and using the same high-quality instructional materials in all cases. Successful high-poverty schools that already had evidence-based instructional strategies and high-quality instructional materials in place before the pandemic might be ready to start integrating tutoring into their programs. But other schools have to walk before they can run.

- **Build a positive and supportive school climate.** Many students have returned to school with significant mental health needs. Some have experienced significant trauma associated variously with the pandemic, economic downturn, and America's reckoning with racial injustice. This will lead some students to act out or shut down at school. By building strong relationships, ensuring school policies and practices reflect and engage diverse families, and setting high, common, school-wide expectations for behavior and academic achievement, schools can help students feel safe and optimistic and keep them focused on learning.

- **Don't bite off more than you can chew.** The only recommendations that will help students thrive are ones that are implemented thoughtfully, with fidelity, and with attention to detail. Aim for quality over quantity, and save some steps for later.

- **Make teachers' jobs doable.** Consider asking teachers to team up via departmentalization, for example, with one teaching English language arts and another teaching mathematics to both of their classrooms. That may be especially helpful at schools that are implementing new high-quality curricula, since each teacher would have fewer subjects to master. Alternatively, schools with several years of experience with high-quality instructional materials might consider "looping," where teachers stay with their current students and follow them into the next grade in the fall, in order to maintain strong relationships. All schools, districts, and networks should also consider focusing on priority instructional content as identified by Student Achievement Partners.[174]

- **Embrace external support.** Most schools should get help from professional learning organizations with expertise in the high-quality curricula their district or network has chosen. Such curricula come with embedded assessments that produce actionable data. External support organizations can help schools and teachers make good decisions around mid-course corrections.

Additional considerations for school improvement efforts

- Understand that the technical and social aspects of school improvement work are of equal importance.

- Apply the principles of systems thinking to school improvement work: "shift from viewing education as a system in which one teacher provides information to many students toward a system in which there are many information resources accessible by one student, only one of which is the teacher. This shift can accurately be characterized as moving from an emphasis on instruction to an emphasis on learning."[175]

Finally, we note a recent review of research of implementation fidelity and failures by Anna Erickson and Heather Hill.[176] In their review, they found four common elements from qualitative studies that help determine whether programs succeed or fall flat:[177]

- **Will:** Whether teachers actually use new materials.

- **Skill:** Whether teachers know how to use new materials.

- **Organizational capacity:** Whether an organization has the tools, routines, and relationships necessary to use new materials.

- **Contexts and coherence:** Whether new materials are aligned to the local settings' needs, strengths, and weaknesses

Sample student schedule

A school's precise schedule will depend on the time requirements for its chosen curriculum, along with various constraints, such as collective bargaining agreements and transportation logistics. Those specifics aside, here's one example of a schedule that makes room for all of the elements discussed in this volume.

9:00	Arrival/Breakfast	
9:15	Morning Meeting	
9:30 9:45 10:00 10:15 10:30 10:45 11:00 11:15	English Language Arts 120 min	
11:30 11:45	History/Geography 30 min	
12:00 12:15 12:30	Recess/Lunch 45 min	Teachers off duty
12:45 1:00 1:15 1:30	Math 60 min	
1:45 2:00	Science 30 min	
2:15 2:30 2:45	Art, Music, PE, Counseling, Library 45 min	Teachers: Planning, PLC time
3:00 3:15 3:30 3:45	Extended Learning Time - High-dosage tutoring - Enrichment activities	Teachers off duty

APPENDIX
ACKNOWLEDGMENTS

We cannot thank our reviewers enough for their insights and improvements. Together, they have recommended more than 1000 changes to this document to date.

REVIEWERS

Name	Title	Organization
Wendi Anderson	Director of Humanities	CenterPoint Education Solutions
Amy Briggs	President	Student Achievement Partners
Susan Pimentel	Founding Partner	Student Achievement Partners
Paul Bruno	Assistant Professor of Education Policy, Organization and Leadership	University of Illinois
Amber Burks-Cole	District Relationship Manager	CenterPoint Education Solutions
Michele Caracappa	Chief Program Officer	New Leaders
Bailey Cato Czupryk	Vice President	TNTP
Corinne Colgan	Chief of Teaching and Learning	DCPS
Chris Curran	Associate Professor of Educational Leadership and Policy	University of Florida
John Davis	Chief of Schools	Baltimore Public Schools
Chrys Dougherty	Program Director, Division of Strategic Planning and Funding	Texas Higher Ed Board
John A. Dues	Chief Learning Officer	United Schools Network
Tracy Epp	Chief Academic Officer	Richmond Public Schools
Emily Freitag	Co-founder and CEO	Instruction Partners
Seth Gershenson	Associate Professor of Public Administration and Policy	American University
Daniel Gohl	Chief Academic Officer	Broward County Public Schools
Mike Goldstein	Founder	Match Education (former)
Derek Gottlieb	Assistant Professor of Teacher Education	University of Northern Colorado
Sofoklis Goulas	Senior Research Analyst	CREDO at Stanford
Mary Alice Heuschel	Deputy Director for K–12 Education, US Program	Bill & Melinda Gates Foundation
Nate Jensen	Director of the Center for School and Student Progress	NWEA

Name	Title	Organization
Eric Kalenze	US Ambassador	researchED
Rebecca Kockler	Assistant Superintendent of Academic Content	Louisiana Department of Education (former)
Matt Kraft	Associate Professor of Education and Economics	Brown University
Doug Lemov	Managing Director	Uncommon Schools
Kim Marshall	Founder	Marshall Memo
Jared Myracle	Chief Academic Officer	Jackson-Madison County School System (former)
Jamila Newman	Partner	TNTP
Brian Pick	Doctoral Resident	Chicago Public Schools
Gene Pinkard	Director, Practice and Leadership	Aspen Institute
Morgan Polikoff	Associate Professor of Education	University of Southern California
Ricki Price-Baugh	Director of Academic Achievement	Council of Great City Schools
Benjamin Riley	Founder and Executive Director	Deans for Impact
Robert Schwartz	Chief Academic Officer	ICEF (former)
Irvin Scott	Senior Lecturer on Education	Harvard Graduate School of Education
Arnold Shober	Professor of Government	Lawrence University
Katie Shuman	Curriculum Specialist	CenterPoint Education Solutions
Laura Slover	CEO	CenterPoint Education Solutions
Lindsey Smith	Chief Academic Officer	Attuned
Sabrina Solanki	Institute of Education Sciences Postdoctoral Fellow	University of Michigan
Jamie Spears	Senior Manager, Mathematics & Special Education	TNTP
Matthew Steinberg	Associate Professor of Education Policy	George Mason University
David Steiner	Director for the Institute for Education Policy	Johns Hopkins University
Jessica Sutter	President	EdPro Consulting

Name	Title	Organization
Laura Sztejnberg	Director of Research and Senior Program Officer	Overdeck Family Foundation
Vivian Tseng	Senior Vice President, Program	WT Grant Foundation
Sivan Tuchman	Research Analyst	Center on Reinventing Public Education
Remy Washington	Chief Academic Officer	Uplift Education
Joey Webb	Director of Academic Services	CenterPoint Education Solutions
Natalie Wexler	Author	*The Knowledge Gap*
Alyssa Whitehead-Bust	Partner	Attuned
Dylan Wiliam	Emeritus Professor of Educational Assessment	UCL Institute of Education
Jason Zimba	Founding Partner	Student Achievement Partners

ANNOTATED BIBLIOGRAPHY

A

Achievement First. "Supporting intellectual lift in planning & execution – math." 2018. https://www.achievementfirst.org/wp-content/uploads/2018/02/Intellectual_Prep_Protocol_AF_2014.docx.

ACT. "Reading between the lines: What the ACT reveals about college readiness in reading." Iowa City, IA: ACT, 2006. https://www.act.org/content/dam/act/unsecured/documents/reading_summary.pdf.

- The ability to handle complex text is connected to meeting the College Readiness Benchmark on the ACT Reading exam, which in other research is connected to success in specific college courses.

Adams, Marilyn J., Lily Wong Fillmore, Claude Goldenberg, Jane Oakhill, David D. Paige, Timothy Rasinski, and Timothy Shanahan. "Comparing reading research to program design: An examination of teachers college units of study." New York, NY: Student Achievement Partners, 2020. https://achievethecore.org/page/3240/comparing-reading-research-to-program-design-an-examination-of-teachers-college-units-of-study.

- Outlines how the Teachers College Units of Study ELA curriculum is not aligned to the Common Core, in particular due to its lack of attention to knowledge-building.

Akerson, Valarie and Lisa A. Donnelly. "Teaching nature of science to K–2 students: What understandings can they attain?" *International Journal of Science Education* 32, no. 1 (2010): 1–28. https://doi.org/10.1080/09500690902717283.

Akerson, Valarie, Gayle A. Buck, Lisa A. Donnelly, Vanashri Nargund-Joshi, and Ingrid S. Weiland. "The importance of teaching and learning nature of science in the early childhood years." *Journal of Science Education and Technology* 20 (May 2011): 537–49. https://doi.org/10.1007/s10956-011-9312-5.

Ali, Mir M., Kristina West, Judith L. Teich, Sean Lynch, Ryan Mutter, and Joel Dubenitz. "Utilization of mental health services in educational setting by adolescents in the United States." *Journal of School Health* 89, no. 5 (March 2019): 393–401. https://doi.org/10.1111/josh.12753.

Allensworth, Elaine and Nate Schwartz. "School practices to address student learning loss." Brief No. 1, EdResearch for Recovery Project. Annenberg Institute at Brown University, Results for America, June 2020. https://annenberg.brown.edu/sites/default/files/EdResearch_for_Recovery_Brief_1.pdf.

- This useful and succinct policy brief outlines key rationales for and promising strategies to implement high-dosage tutoring programs.

Alsalamah, Areej. "The effectiveness of providing reading instruction via Tier 2 of Response to Intervention." *International Journal of Research in Humanities & Social Sciences* 5, no. 3 (March 2017): 6–17. https://www.researchgate.net/publication/317519024_The_Effectiveness_of_Providing_Reading_Instruction_Via_Tier_2_of_Response_to_Intervention.

- Studies of Tier 2 instruction have not been done on schools where Tier 1 instruction is necessarily strong.

American School Counselor Association (ASCA), National Association of School Psychologists (NASP). *School reentry considerations: Supporting student social and emotional learning and mental and behavioral health amidst Covid-19.* n.d. https://www.schoolcounselor.org/getmedia/44fe18dc-6a97-4644-950d-0799d94caaa1/School-Reentry.pdf.

Anderson, Richard C., Elfrieda H. Hiebert, Judith A. Scott, Ian A. G. Wilkinson, Wes Becker, and Wesley C. Becker. "Becoming a nation of readers: The report of the commission on reading." *Education and Treatment of Children* 11, no. 4 (1988): 389–96. http://www.jstor.org/stable/42899086.

- Cited here as the source of concerns about the differences in how lower-level and higher-level students are engaged by teachers.

Arnold, Kathleen, Sharda Umanath, Kara Thio, Walter B. Reilly, Mark A. McDaniel, and Elizabeth J. Marsh. "Understanding the cognitive processes involved in writing to learn." *Journal of Experimental Psychology: Applied* 23, no. 2 (2017): 115–27. https://doi.org/10.1037/xap0000119.

Ashman, Greg. *The power of explicit teaching and direct instruction.* Thousand Oaks, CA: Corwin, 2020. http://us.sagepub.com/en-us/nam/the-power-of-explicit-teaching-and-direct-instruction/book273757#contents.

Aspen Institute. *Integrating Social, Emotional, and Academic Development (SEAD): An action guide for school leadership teams.* Washington, DC: National Commission on Social, Emotional, and Academic Development, 2019. https://www.aspeninstitute.org/publications/integrating-social-emotional-and-academic-development-sead-an-action-guide-for-school-leadership-teams/.

Aspen Institute. *Putting it all together.* Washington, DC: National Commission on Social, Emotional, and Academic Development, 2017. https://www.aspeninstitute.org/publications/putting-it-all-together/.

Atkinson, Robert K., Sharon J. Derry, Alexander Renkl, and Donald Wortham. "Learning from examples: Instructional principles from the worked examples research." *Review of Educational Research* 70, no. 2 (June 2000): 181–214. https://doi.org/10.3102/00346543070002181.

- Curricula that include multiple worked examples for math problems are effective at promoting conceptual understanding.

B

Baicker, Karen. "The impact of secondary trauma on educators." *Stress-Busting Strategies for Educators* 15, no. 13 (March 2020). https://www.ascd.org/el/articles/the-impact-of-secondary-trauma-on-educators.

Baker, Scott, Nonie Lesaux, Madhavi Jayanthi, Joseph Dimino, C. Patrick Proctor, Joan Morris, Russell Gersten, Kelly Haymond, Michael J. Kieffer, Sylvia Linan-Thompson, and Rebecca Newman-Gonchar. *Teaching academic content and literacy to English learners in elementary and middle school.* NCEE 2014-4012. Washington, DC: US Department of Education, Institute of Education Sciences, National Center for Education Evaluation and Regional Assistance, April 2014. https://ies.ed.gov/ncee/wwc/PracticeGuide/19.

Balfanz, Robert and Vaughan Byrnes. "Using data and the human touch: Evaluating the NYC inter-agency campaign to reduce chronic absenteeism." *Journal of Education for Students Placed at Risk (JESPAR)* 23, no. 1-2 (2018): 107–21. https://doi.org/10.1080/10824669.2018.1435283.

Bangert-Drowns, Robert L., Marlene M. Hurley, and Barbara Wilkinson. "The effects of school-based writing-to-learn interventions on academic achievement: A meta-analysis." *Review of Educational Research* 74, no. 1 (March 2004): 29–58. https://doi.org/10.3102/00346543074001029.

Barbarasch, Barry, and Elias, Maurice J. "Fostering social competence in schools." In *School-based mental health: A practitioner's guide to comparative practices,* edited by Ray W. Christner and Rosemary B. Mennuti, 125–148. New York, NY: Routledge/Taylor & Francis Group, 2009.

- Points to many possible benefits of SEL, including developing a sense of citizenship.

Bath, Howard. "The three pillars of trauma-informed care." *Reclaiming Children and Youth* 17, no. 3 (Fall 2008): 17–21. https://eric.ed.gov/?id=EJ869920.

Bauer, Lauren, Stephanie Lu, and Emily Moss. "Teen disengagement is on the rise." *Up Front* (blog), Brookings Institution, October 1, 2020. https://www.brookings.edu/blog/up-front/2020/10/01/teen-disengagement-is-on-the-rise/.

Baye, Ariane, Amanda Inns, Cynthia Lake, and Robert E. Slavin. "A synthesis of quantitative research on reading programs for secondary students." *International Literacy Association Reading Research Quarterly* 54, no. 2 (2018): 133–166. https://doi.org/10.1002/rrq.229.

- This review of experimental research identifies categories of programs that show positive outcomes on widely accepted measures of reading, one-to-one and small-group tutoring being among them.

Betts, Frank. "How systems thinking applies to education." *Educational Leadership* 50, no. 3 (November 1992). http://www.ascd.org/publications/educational-leadership/nov92/vol50/num03/How-Systems-Thinking-Applies-to-Education.aspx.

Bhatt, Rachana, Cory Koedel, and Douglas Lehmann. "Is curriculum quality uniform? Evidence from Florida." *Economics of Education Review* 34 (June 2013): 107–21. https://doi.org/10.1016/j.econedurev.2013.01.014.

- Textbook choice has statistically significant effects on test scores, this evaluation of curricular effectiveness in elementary mathematics finds.

Black, Paul, and Dylan Wiliam. "Assessment and classroom learning." *Assessment in Education* 5, no. 1 (July 1998): 7–74. https://doi.org/10.1080/0969595980050102.

- Feedback should be rapid so that students still remember the task and the skills when they were being assessed.

Blanding, Michael. "Treating the 'instructional core': Education rounds." Harvard University, Graduate School of Education, May 12, 2009. https://www.gse.harvard.edu/news/uk/09/05/treating-instructional-core-education-rounds.

Blank, Rolf K. "Science instructional time is declining in elementary schools: What are the implications for student achievement and closing the gap?" *Science Education* 97, no. 6 (October 2013): 830–47. https://doi.org/10.1002/sce.21078.

- Curriculum selection has large and statistically significant effects on student outcomes, rivaling teacher effectiveness interventions.

Briars, Diane, and Lauren Resnick. *Standards assessments—and what else? The essential elements of standards-based school improvement*. Los Angeles, CA: The National Center for Research on Evaluation, Standards, and Student Testing, January 2000. https://www.researchgate.net/publication/234582727_Standards_Assessments--and_What_Else_The_Essential_Elements_of_Standards-Based_School_Improvement_CSE_Technical_Report.

Brown, Peter C., Henry L. Roediger and Mark A. McDaniel. *Make it stick: The science of successful learning*. Cambridge, MA: The Belknap Press of Harvard University Press, 2014.

- The book is a "must-read" for anyone interested in the science of learning.

Brunner, Cornelia, Chad Fasca, Juliette Heinze, Margaret Honey, Daniel Light, Ellen Mardinach, and Dara Wexler. "Linking data and learning: The Grow Network study." *Journal of Education for Students Placed at Risk* 10, no. 3 (2005): 241–67. https://doi.org/10.1207/s15327671espr1003_2.

- Feedback should provide concrete information and suggestions for improvement.

Bryk, Anthony S., Louis M. Gomez, Alicia Grunow, and Paul G. LeMahieu. *Learning to improve: How America's schools can get better at getting better*. Cambridge, MA: Harvard Education Press, 2015.

Bryk, Anthony S., Penny Bender Sebring, Elaine Allensworth, Stuart Luppescu, and John Q. Easton. *Organizing schools for improvement: Lessons from Chicago*. Chicago: The University of Chicago Press, 2010.

Bryk, Anthony S., Valerie E. Lee, and Peter B. Holland. *Catholic schools and the common good*. Cambridge: Harvard University Press, 1995.

Bunch, George, Amanda Kibler, and Susan Pimentel. *Realizing opportunities for ELs in the Common Core English Language Arts and Disciplinary Literacy Standards*. Presented at the annual meeting of the Understanding Language Conference, January 2012.

C

Cabell, Sonia Q., and HyeJin Hwang. "Building content knowledge to boost comprehension in the primary grades." *Reading Research Quarterly* 55, no. 1 (August 2020), 99–107. http://dx.doi.org/10.1002/rrq.338.

- Discusses why content-rich instruction supports language and content acquisition and improves linguistic and reading comprehension. Also shares preliminary results of an IES study of the Core Knowledge English Language Arts curriculum.

California State University, Los Angeles, Charter College of Education. "Improving instruction, accessibility, and outcomes." Accessed November 18, 2021. https://ceedar. education.ufl.edu/mtss-udl-di-dev/.

Carlana, Michela, and Eliana La Ferrara. *Apart but connected: Online tutoring and student outcomes during the COVID-19 pandemic.* EdWorkingPaper 21-350. Providence: Annenberg Institute at Brown University, February 2021. https://doi. org/10.26300/0azm-cf65.

- A virtual tutoring program implemented in Italian middle schools during the early months of the Covid pandemic substantially increased academic performance, socio-emotional skills, aspirations, and psychological wellbeing. These effects were greater for children from lower socioeconomic backgrounds and for immigrant children.

Carpenter, Shana K., Harold Pashler, John T. Wixted, and Edward Vul. "The effects of tests on learning and forgetting." *Memory & Cognition* 36 (January 2008): 438–48. https://doi.org/10.3758/MC.36.2.438.

- Findings confirm that testing enhanced overall recall more than restudying did.

Carter Andrews, Dorinda J. and Melissa Gutwein. "'Maybe that concept is still with us': Adolescents' racialized and classed perceptions of teachers' expectations." *Multicultural Perspectives* 19, no. 1 (2017): 5–15. https://doi.org/10.1080/15210960.2016.1263960.

- Demonstrates the baseline principle that teachers' expectations for students have a significant effect on academic achievement.

Castles, Anne, Kathleen Rastle, and Kate Nation. "Ending the reading wars: Reading acquisition from novice to expert." *Psychological Science in the Public Interest* 19, no. 1 (June 2018): 5–51. https://doi.org/10.1177/1529100618772271.

CenterPoint Education Solutions. "Aligning curriculum and assessments to advance achievement with CenterPoint and EL Education." Washington DC, February 11, 2020. https://centerpointeducation.org/news-events/_aligning_curriculum_and_assessment.

Cepeda, Nicholas J., Harold Pashler, Edward Vul, John T. Wixted, and Doug Rohrer. "Distributed practice in verbal recall tasks: A review and quantitative synthesis." *Psychological Bulletin* 132, no. 3 (2006): 354–80. https://doi.org/10.1037/0033-2909.132.3.354.

- Contains a review and quantitative synthesis of hundreds of experiments on the effects of massed versus distributed practice.

Chenoweth, Karin. *"It's being done": Academic success in unexpected schools.* Cambridge, MA: Harvard Education Press, 2007.

Chiefs for Change and Johns Hopkins University Institute for Education Policy. "How should education leaders prepare for reentry and beyond?" May 2020. https://chiefsforchange.org/wp-content/uploads/2020/06/CFC-TheReturn_5-13-20.pdf.

Chin, Mark J., David M. Quinn, Tasminda K. Dhaliwal, and Virginia S. Lovison. "Bias in the air: A nationwide exploration of teachers' implicit racial attitudes, aggregate bias, and student outcomes." *Educational Researcher* 49, no. 8 (November 2020): 566–78. https://doi.org/10.3102/0013189X20937240.

Chingos, Matthew M. and Grover R. Whitehurst. *Choosing blindly: Instructional materials, teacher effectiveness, and the Common Core.* Washington, DC: Brookings Institution, April 2012. https://www.brookings.edu/wp-content/uploads/2016/06/0410_curriculum_chingos_whitehurst.pdf.

Collaborative for Academic, Social, and Emotional Learning (CASEL). *Social and Emotional Learning (SEL) and student benefits: Implications for the safe schools/healthy students core elements.* Chicago, IL: CASEL, 2008. https://eric.ed.gov/?id=ED505369.

- Well-implemented SEL programs can have positive impacts on students' academic, behavioral and health outcomes.

Common Core. *Why we're behind: What top nations teach their student but we don't.* Washington, DC: Common Core, 2009. https://www.giarts.org/sites/default/files/Why-Were-Behind.pdf.

- Common Core, the precursor to Great Minds, found commonalities among the diverse countries with the highest PISA scores: education systems that emphasize content knowledge in academic standards, curriculum, and assessments.

Cook, Philip, Kenneth Dodge, George Farkas, Roland Fryer, Jonathan Guryan, Jens Ludwig, Susan Mayer, Harold Pollack, and Laurence Steinberg. *The (surprising) efficacy of academic and behavioral intervention with disadvantaged youth: Results from a randomized experiment in Chicago.* NBER Working Paper 19862. Cambridge: National Bureau of Economic Research, January 2014. https://doi.org/10.3386/w19862.

Cooper, Graham, and John Sweller. "The effects of schema acquisition and rule automation on mathematical problem-solving transfer." *Journal of Educational Psychology* 79, no. 4 (1987): 347–62. https://doi.org/10.1037/0022-0663.79.4.347.

- When lessons teach students the concepts (schema) under certain math rules, students' conceptual understanding and fluency are improved.

Council of Chief State School Officers (CCSSO). "The marginalization of social studies." November 16, 2018. https://ccsso.org/resource-library/marginalization-social-studies.

Cranston, Jerome. "Relational trust: The glue that binds a professional learning community." *Alberta Journal of Educational Research* 57, no. 1 (Spring): 59–72. https://eric.ed.gov/?id=EJ934010.

Cultivating Awareness and Resilience in Education (CARE). "Research findings on Care." Accessed November 18, 2021. https://createforeducation.org/care/care-research/.

Curran, Chris F., and James Kitchin. "Early elementary science instruction: Does more time on science or science topics/skills predict science achievement in the early grades?" *AERA Open* 5, no. 3 (July–September 2019): 1–18. https://doi.org/10.1177/2332858419861081.

- More time spent on science topics correlates with higher science achievement in elementary school. This speaks to an idea that should not be taken for granted: spending more time on science leads to higher levels of achievement.

D

Daly, Brian, Cindy Buchanan, Kimberly Dasch, Dawn Eichen, and Clare Lenhart. "Promoting school connectedness among urban youth of color: Reducing risk factors while promoting protective factors." *The prevention researcher* 17 (2010): 18–21. https://doi.org/10.1037/e597072010-006.

Darling-Hammond, Linda, Maria E. Hyler, and Madelyn Gardner. *Effective teacher professional development.* Palo Alto, CA: Learning Policy Institute, June 5, 2017. https://learningpolicyinstitute.org/product/effective-teacher-professional-development-report.

Davis-Kean, Pamela. "The influence of parent education and family income on child achievement: The indirect role of parental expectations and the home environment." *Journal of Family Psychology* 19, no. 2 (2005): 294–304. http://dx.doi.org/10.1037/0893-3200.19.2.294.

de Boer, Hester, Anneke C. Timmermans, and Margaretha P. C. van der Werf. "The effects of teacher expectation interventions on teachers' expectations and student achievement: Narrative review and meta-analysis." *Educational Research and Evaluation* 24, no. 3–5 (2018): 180–200. http://dx.doi.org/10.1080/13803611.2018.1550834.

- Clarifies the concept of high expectations, specifically that students recognize when teachers have high expectations for them, which relates to stronger performance.

Delpit, Lisa. *"Multiplication is for White people": Raising expectations for other people's children.* New York, NY: The New Press, 2012.

Deming, W. Edwards. *The new economics for industry, government, education.* 3rd. Ed. Cambridge, MA: MIT Press, 2018.

Dettmers, Swantje, Sittipan Yotyodying, and Kathrin Jonkmann. "Antecedents and outcomes of parental homework involvement: How do family-school partnerships affect parental homework involvement and student outcomes?" *Frontiers in Psychology* 10, no. 1048 (May 2019). https://doi.org/10.3389/fpsyg.2019.01048.

- Simply assigning a lot of homework does not necessarily lead to its being completed. Robust family engagement (family–school partnerships in a German context) leads to improved homework completion.

DeWitt, Sharon. "The effects of note taking and mental rehearsal on memory." *Journal of Undergraduate Psychological Research* 2 (2007): 46–9. http://library.wcsu.edu/dspace/bitstream/0/65/1/dewitt.pdf.

Dietrichson, Jens, Martin Bøg, Trine Filges, and Anne-Marie Klint Jørgensen. "Academic interventions for elementary and middle school students with low socioeconomic status: A systematic review and meta-analysis." *Review of Educational Research* 87, no. 2 (April 2017): 243–82. https://doi.org/10.3102/0034654316687036.

- This meta-analysis reveals tutoring to be a highly effective educational strategy for low-socioeconomic status students, followed closely by feedback and progress monitoring.

Dinnen, Hannah, Morgan Cody, Emily Jordan and Cricket Meehan. "Referral pathways protocol for mental health supports." Project AWARE Ohio, n. d. https://www.escneo.org/Downloads/Referral-Pathways-Protocol-for-Mental-Health-Supports-FINAL2.pdf.

District of Columbia Public Schools (DCPS). *LEAP: Teacher professional development.* Accessed November 16, 2021. https://dcps.dc.gov/page/leap-teacher-professional-development.

Dogan, Selcuk, Rose Pringle, and Jennifer Mesa. "The impacts of professional learning communities on science teachers' knowledge, practice and student learning: A review." *Professional Development in Education* 42, no. 4 (2015): 569–88. http://dx.doi.org/10.1080/19415257.2015.1065899.

- Reviews empirical studies on the impact of PLCs on the practice and knowledge of K–12 science teachers, specifically examining changes in disciplinary content knowledge and pedagogical content knowledge, and found that PLCs can help teachers increase both types of knowledge.

Durlak, Joseph A., Roger P. Weissberg, Allison B. Dymnicki, Rebecca D. Taylor, and Kriston B. Schellinger. "The impact of enhancing students' social and emotional learning: A meta-analysis of school-based universal interventions." *Child Development* 82, no. 1 (January–February 2011): 405–32. https://doi.org/10.1111/j.1467-8624.2010.01564.x.

- Meta-analysis that points to clear academic and behavioral benefits for students in schools that have undertaken SEL interventions. A significant, positive impact on a range of outcomes is associated with a variety of interventions.

E

EdReports. "Amplify science." Accessed November 17, 2021. https://www.edreports.org/reports/overview/amplify-science-2018.

EdReports. *Core Knowledge Language Arts (CKLA) (2015)*. Accessed November 17, 2021. https://www.edreports.org/reports/overview/core-knowledge-language-arts-ckla-2015.

Education Reform Now, The Education Trust, and FutureEd. "Report: State guidance for high-impact tutoring." May 26, 2021. https://edreformnow.org/policy-briefs/report-state-guidance-for-high-impact-tutoring/.

Education Resource Strategies (ERS). "Unit unpacking to methodically drive student achievement." https://www.erstrategies.org/cms/files/3504-unit-unpacking-protocol.pdf.

Education Trust and MDRC. "Targeted intensive tutoring." March 17, 2021. https://edtrust.org/resource/targeted-intensive-tutoring/.

Education World. *School mission statements: Where is your school going?* Education World. Accessed November 24, 2021. https://www.educationworld.com/a_admin/admin/admin229.shtml.

Elleman, Amy M., Endia J. Lindo, Paul Morphy, and Donald L. Compton. "The impact of vocabulary instruction on passage-level comprehension of school-age children: A meta-analysis." *Journal of Research on Educational Effectiveness* 2, no. 1 (2009): 1–44. https://doi.org/10.1080/19345740802539200.

- Teaching explicit vocabulary, which is a major component of history and science curricula, has a positive impact on reading comprehension.

Elmore, Richard. *Bridging the gap between standards and achievement: The imperative for professional development in education.* Washington, DC: Albert Shanker Institute, 2002. https://www.shankerinstitute.org/resource/bridging-gap-between-standards-and-achievement.

- Student learning depends on the relationships established between a teacher, their students, and the content, which is defined as the "instructional core." Attention to all three is essential for improved student outcomes.

Epstein, Michael, Marc Atkins, Douglas Cullinan, Krista Kutash, and Robin Weaver. *Reducing behavior problems in the elementary school classroom: A practice guide.* NCEE #2008-012. Washington, DC: US Department of Education, Institute of Education Sciences, National Center for Education Evaluation and Regional Assistance, September 2008. https://ies.ed.gov/ncee/wwc/PracticeGuide/4.

- Provides the evidence base for the idea that clear rules and expectations that are reinforced deliberately by teachers improve student behavior.

F

Ferlazzo, Larry. "The what, why, and how of 'interleaving'," *Education Week*, May 30, 2021. https://www.edweek.org/teaching-learning/opinion-the-what-why-how-of-interleaving/2021/05.

Fincher-Kiefer, Rebecca. "The role of prior knowledge in inferential processing." *Journal of Research in Reading* 15, no. 1 (1992): 12–27. https://doi.org/10.1111/j.1467-9817.1992.tb00018.x.

- Students with background knowledge of a particular subject are better equipped to figure out the meaning of unknown words connected to a corresponding domain of knowledge. This suggests that giving students a broad knowledge base in elementary school will better prepare them to learn new vocabulary in middle and high school.

Frye, Douglas, Arthur J. Baroody, Margaret Burchinal, Sharon M. Carver, Nancy C. Jordan, and Judy McDowell. *Teaching math to young children: A practice guide.* NCEE 2014-4005. Washington, DC: US Department of Education, Institute of Education Sciences, National Center for Education Evaluation and Regional Assistance, 2013. https://ies.ed.gov/ncee/wwc/PracticeGuide/18.

Fryer, Roland G. "Injecting charter school best practices into traditional public schools: Evidence from field experiments." *The Quarterly Journal of Economics* 129, no. 3 (2014): 1355–407. https://scholar.harvard.edu/files/fryer/files/2014_injecting_charter_school_best_practices_into_traditional_public_schools.pdf.

Fryer, Roland G. *The production of human capital in developed countries: Evidence from 196 randomized field experiments.* NBER Working Paper 22130. Cambridge, MA: National Bureau of Economic Research, March 2016. https://doi.org/10.3386/w22130.

- This meta-analysis reviews nearly 200 field experiments to identify the relative impacts of a variety of interventions on educational outcomes. High-dosage tutoring generates the most substantial and consistent academic benefit to students.

Fuchs, Lynn S., Rebecca Newman-Gonchar, Robin Schumacher, Barbara Dougherty, Nicole Bucka, Karen S. Karp, John Woodward, Ben Clarke, Nancy C. Jordan, Russell Gersten, Madhavi Jayanthi et al. *Assisting students struggling with mathematics: Intervention in the elementary grades.* WWC 2021006. Washington, DC: US Department of Education, Institute of Education Sciences, National Center for Education Evaluation and Regional Assistance, 2021. https://ies.ed.gov/ncee/wwc/PracticeGuide/26#tab-summary.

G

Gabriel, John G., and Paul C. Farmer. *How to help your school thrive without breaking the bank.* Alexandria, VA: Association for Supervision and Curriculum Development (ASCD), 2009.

Garcia, Maria Elena, Kay Frunzi, Ceri B. Dean, Nieves Flores, and Kirsten B. Miller. *Toolkit of resources for engaging amilies and the community as partners in education: Part 1: Building an understanding of family and community engagement.* REL 2016–148. Washington, DC: US Department of Education, Institute of Education Sciences, National Center for Education Evaluation and Regional Assistance, Regional Educational Laboratory Pacific, September 2016. https://ies.ed.gov/ncee/edlabs/projects/project.asp?projectID=4509.

- Speaks to the importance of sharing data with families about how their children are doing in a meaningful way as a key part of a family engagement strategy.

Gershenson, Seth. "Linking teacher quality, student attendance, and student achievement." *Education Finance and Policy* 11, no. 2 (Spring 2016): 125–49. http://dx.doi.org/10.1162/EDFP_a_00180.

Gershenson, Seth and Nicholas Papageorge. "The power of teacher expectations." *Education Next* 18, no. 1 (2017). https://www.educationnext.org/power-of-teacher-expectations-racial-bias-hinders-student-attainment/.

Gersten, Russell, Sybilla Beckmann, Benjamin Clarke, Anne Foegen, Laurel Marsh, Jon R. Star, and Bradley Witzel. *Assisting students struggling with mathematics: Response to Intervention (RtI) for elementary and middle schools.* NCEE 2009-4060. Washington, DC: US Department of Education, Institute of Education Sciences, National Center for Education Evaluation and Regional Assistance, April 2009. https://ies.ed.gov/ncee/wwc/PracticeGuide/2.

Gersten, Russell, Donald Compton, Carol M. Connor, Joseph Dimino, Lana Santoro, Sylvia Linan-Thompson, and W. David Tilly. *Assisting students struggling with reading: Response to Intervention (RtI) and multi-tier intervention in the primary grades.* NCEE 2009-4045. Washington, DC: US Department of Education, Institute of Education Sciences, National Center for Education Evaluation and Regional Assistance, February 2009. https://ies.ed.gov/ncee/wwc/PracticeGuide/3.

Ginsburg, Alan, Geneise Cooke, Steve Leinwand, Jay Noell, and Elizabeth Pollock.

Reassessing U.S. international mathematics performance: New findings from the 2003 TIMSS and PISA. Washington, DC: American Institutes for Research, November 2005. https://files.eric.ed.gov/fulltext/ED491624.pdf.

- Finds no evidence of a sharp decline by US students on PISA compared with TIMSS.

Goldenberg, Claude. "Teaching English language learners." *American Educator* (Summer 2008): 8–23, 42–44. https://www.aft.org/sites/default/files/periodicals/goldenberg.pdf.

Goldenberg, Claude. "Unlocking the research on English learners." *American Educator* (Summer 2013): 4–11. https://dataworks-ed.com/wp-content/uploads/2016/05/Goldenberg.pdf.

Goldstein, Michael and Bowen Paulle. *The narrow path to do it right: Lessons from vaccine making for high-dosage tutoring.* Washington DC: Thomas B. Fordham Institute, March 2021. https://fordhaminstitute.org/national/research/narrow-path-do-it-right-lessons-vaccine-making-high-dosage-tutoring.

Graham, Steve, Alisha Bollinger, Carol Booth Olson, Catherine D'Aoust, Charles MacArthur, Deborah McCutchen, and Natalie Olinghouse. *Teaching elementary school students to be effective writers: A practice guide.* NCEE 2012-4058. Washington, DC: US Department of Education, Institute of Education Sciences, National Center for Education Evaluation and Regional Assistance, 2012. https://ies.ed.gov/ncee/wwc/PracticeGuide/17.

Graham, Steve, and Michael Hebert. *Writing to read: Evidence for how writing can improve reading.* A report to Carnegie Corporation of New York. Washington, DC: Alliance for Excellent Education, 2010. https://www.carnegie.org/publications/writing-to-read-evidence-for-how-writing-can-improve-reading/.

- Teaching sentence-construction skills has improved reading fluency and comprehension.

Graham, Steve, Sharlene A. Kiuhara, and Meade MacKay. "The effects of writing on learning in science, social studies, and mathematics: A meta-analysis." *Review of Educational Research* 90, no. 2 (April 2020): 179–226. http://dx.doi.org/10.3102/0034654320914744.

- Embedding writing instruction in content and having students write about what they are learning in English language arts, social studies, science, and math has boosted reading comprehension and learning across grade levels.

Graham, Steve, and Dolores Perin. *Writing next: Effective strategies to improve writing of adolescents in middle and high schools.* A report to Carnegie Corporation of New York. Washington, DC: Alliance for Excellent Education, 2007. https://www.carnegie.org/publications/writing-next-effective-strategies-to-improve-writing-of-adolescents-in-middle-and-high-schools/.

Greenberg, Julie, Hannah Putman, and Kate Walsh. *Training our future teachers: Classroom Management.* Washington DC: National Council on Teacher Quality, January 2014. https://www.nctq.org/dmsView/Future_Teachers_Classroom_Management_NCTQ_Report.

- Draws heavily on research-backed classroom management practices and identifies five key strategies that teacher candidates should master: establish rules, build routines, reinforce positive behavior, impose consequences for misbehavior, and foster student engagement.

Guilford County Schools. *Opportunity Culture.* Accessed November 18, 2021. https://www.gcsnc.com/Page/43010.

Guskey, Thomas R., and Kwang Suk Yoon. "What works in professional development?" *Phi Delta Kappan* 90, no. 7 (March 2009): 495–500. https://tguskey.com/wp-content/uploads/Professional-Learning-5-What-Works-in-Professional-Development.pdf.

H

Halpern, Diane F., Joshua Aronson, Nona Reimer, Sandra Simpkins, Jon R. Star, and Kathryn Wentzel. *Encouraging girls in math and science.* NCER 2007-2003. Washington, DC: US Department of Education, Institute of Education Sciences, National Center for Education Research, September 2007. https://ies.ed.gov/ncee/wwc/PracticeGuide/5.

Halverson, Richard, Reid B. Prichett, and Jeffrey G. Watson. *Formative feedback systems and the new instructional leadership.* WCER Working Paper. Madison, WI: University of Wisconsin-Madison, 2007. https://eric.ed.gov/?id=ED497265.

Hamilton, Laura, Richard Halverson, Sharnell S. Jackson, Ellen Mandinach, Jonathan A. Supovitz, and Jeffrey C. Wayman. *Using student achievement data to support instructional decision making.* NCEE 2009-4067. Washington, DC: National Center for Education Evaluation and Regional Assistance, Institute of Education Sciences, US Department of Education, September 2009. https://ies.ed.gov/ncee/wwc/practiceguide/12.

Hamre, Bridget K. and Robert C. Pianta. "Can instructional and emotional support in the first-grade classroom make a difference for children at risk of school failure?" *Child Development* 76, no. 5 (2005): 949–67. http://www.jstor.org/stable/3696607.

Hamre, Bridget K. and Robert C. Pianta. "Student-teacher relationships." In *Children's needs III: Development, prevention, and intervention*, edited by George G. Bear and Kathleen M. Minke. Bethesda, MD: National Association of School Psychologists, 2006. https://psycnet.apa.org/record/2006-03571-000.

Hanford, Emily. "At a loss for words: What's wrong with how schools teach reading?" *APM Reports*, August 22, 2019. https://www.apmreports.org/episode/2019/08/22/whats-wrong-how-schools-teach-reading.

Hanford, Emily. "Hard words: Why aren't kids being taught to read?" *APM Reports*, September 10, 2018. https://www.apmreports.org/episode/2018/09/10/hard-words-why-american-kids-arent-being-taught-to-read.

Hanford, Emily. "What the words say: Many kids struggle with reading – and children of color are far less likely to get the help they need." *APM Reports*, August 6, 2020. https://www.apmreports.org/episode/2020/08/06/what-the-words-say.

- These radio documentaries explore why schools have not embraced the science of reading, the ways in which pseudoscientific ideas about literacy have influenced instruction, and the impact on disadvantaged students.

Harvard University, Center for Education Policy Research. "Study finds that curriculum alone does not improve student outcomes." March 11, 2019. https://cepr.harvard.edu/curriculum-press-release.

Harvard University, Graduate School of Education. *Quality work protocol*. Accessed November 16, 2021. https://eleducation.org/resources/quality-work-protocol.

Hassel, Bryan C. and Emily Ayscue Hassel. *Opportunity at the top: How America's best teachers could close the gaps, raise the bar, and keep our nation great*. Chapel Hill, NC: Public Impact, 2010. https://files.eric.ed.gov/fulltext/ED539999.pdf.

Heinrich, Carolyn J., Patricia Burch, Annalee Good, Rudy Acosta, Huiping Cheng, Marcus Dillender, Christi Kirshbaum, Hiren Nisar, and Mary Stewart. "Improving the implementation and effectiveness of out-of-school-time tutoring." *Journal of Policy Analysis and Management* 33, no. 2 (Spring 2014): 471–94. https://doi.org/10.1002/pam.21745.

Hempenstall, Kerry. "The three-cueing system: Trojan horse?" *Australian Journal of Learning Disabilities* 8, no. 2 (2003): 15–23. https://doi.org/10.1080/19404150309546726.

- This study outlines a common yet non-research-backed instructional technique from Australia. The paper points to the pitfalls of how "unfounded but passionately held belief[s]" can have a detrimental impact on the teaching of reading.

Herman, Joan and Barry Gribbons. *Lessons learned in using data to support school inquiry and continuous improvement: Final report to the Stuart Foundation.* Los Angeles, CA: Center for the Study of Evaluation, University of California, Los Angeles, February 2001. https://cresst.org/wp-content/uploads/TR535.pdf.

Hill, Heather C. "Why evidence-backed programs might fall short in your school (and what to do about it)." *Education Week*, May 25, 2021. https://www.edweek.org/leadership/opinion-why-evidence-backed-programs-might-fall-short-in-your-school-and-what-to-do-about-it/2021/05.

Hill, Heather C., and Anna Erickson. "Using implementation fidelity to aid in interpreting program impacts: A brief review." *Educational Researcher* 48, no. 9 (December 2019): 590–98. https://doi.org/10.3102/0013189X19891436.

Hill, Nancy E., Belle Liang, Maggi Price, Whitney Polk, John Perella, and Mandy Savitz-Romer. "Envisioning a meaningful future and academic engagement: The role of parenting practices and school-based relationships." *Psychology in the Schools* 55, no. 6 (June 2018): 595–608. https://doi.org/10.1002/pits.22146.

Hirsch, E. D. "A wealth of words." *City Journal*, Winter 2013. https://www.city-journal.org/html/wealth-words-13523.html.

Hirsch, E. D. *How to educate a citizen: The power of shared knowledge to unify a nation.* New York, NY: Harper Collins, 2020.

Hirsch, E. D. *The knowledge deficit: Closing the shocking education gap for American children.* Boston, MA: Houghton Mifflin, 2007.

Hochman, Judith C. and Natalie Wexler. *The Writing Revolution: A guide to advancing thinking through writing in all subjects and grades.* Hoboken, NJ: Wiley, 2017. https://www.thewritingrevolution.org/.

Hoff, Naphtali. *An analysis of appropriate groupings and recommended strategies and techniques for reading in the classroom.* Independent Study Research Paper, Loyola University, October 2002. https://www.lookstein.org/professional-dev/analysis-appropriate-groupings-recommended-strategies-techniques-reading-classroom/.

- Teachers tend to ask more stimulating questions when working with higher-level students.

Holbein, John B. "Childhood skill development and adult political participation." *American Political Science Review* 111, no. 3 (2017): 572–83. https://doi.org/10.1017/S0003055417000119.

- This 20-year study demonstrates that kindergartners with "psychosocial skills" were more likely to vote in adulthood. The study was based on a childhood random assignment participation in a specific elementary school SEL intervention, The Fast Track Project.

Humphrey, Neil. *Social and emotional learning: A critical appraisal.* Thousand Oaks: CA Sage Publications, 2013. https://eric.ed.gov/?id=ED581709.

- Reviews the many complex factors impacting SEL and implementation. SEL is not a fully crystallized concept that can simply be adopted and implemented.

I

Immordino-Yang, Mary Helen, Linda Darling-Hammond, and Christina Krone. *The brain basis for integrated social, emotional, and academic development: How emotions and social relationships drive learning.* Washington, DC: Aspen Institute, National Commission on Social, Emotional, and Academic Development, 2018. https://eric.ed.gov/?id=ED596337.

- An emotionally safe environment is not only a good in and of itself, but is necessary for student learning.

Instruction Partners. "Addressing unfinished learning in reading." Nashville: Instruction Partners, n.d., https://docs.google.com/presentation/d/16tUJ2vNUy-H2xluEraDi0AopE tRKpr3ZqJYErDICzOA/edit?_hsmi=133205384&_hsenc=p2ANqtz-85KCV8S-0KcOM Pgs7r94RCJm6sxbcVj4YGGGPg17AwaI76rpe744zHb6dOnKZMo_A_RQw-3iWEXywz ExRrTCirYcJ_7QCIJfSypfWZ4S6kmLFKG1E#slide=id.p.

J

Jackson, C. Kirabo and Alexey Makarin. *Can online off-the-shelf lessons improve student outcomes? Evidence from a field experiment.* Working Paper No. 22398. Cambridge, MA: National Bureau of Economic Research, January 2017. https://dx.doi.org/10.3386/w22398.

- The impact of implementing a high-quality curriculum increases when coupled with professional development. While the impact occurs for all teachers, it is largest for the weakest teachers.
- Evidence suggests investments in curriculum components are highly scalable and effects are greatest with weakest teachers, who are disproportionately present in high-needs classrooms.

Jackson, C. Kirabo, Shanette C. Porter, John Q. Easton, Alyssa Blanchard, and Sebastián Kiguel. "School effects on socioemotional development, school-based arrests, and educational attainment." *American Economic Review: Insights* 2, no. 4 (December 2020): 491–508. https://doi.org/10.1257/aeri.20200029.

Jackson, C. Kirabo. *What do test scores miss? The importance of teacher effects on non-test score outcomes.* NBER Working Paper 22226. Cambridge, MA: National Bureau of Economic Research, November 2016. https://doi.org/10.3386/w22226.

Jacob, Brian A., and Jonah E. Rockoff. *Organizing schools to improve student achievement: Start times, grade configurations, and teacher assignments.* Washington, DC: Brookings Institution, September 2011. https://www.brookings.edu/research/organizing-schools-to-improve-student-achievement-start-times-grade-configurations-and-teacher-assignments/.

Jacobs, Victoria R., Megan Loef Franke, Thomas P. Carpenter, Linda Levi, and Dan Battey. "Professional development focused on children's algebraic reasoning in elementary school." *Journal for Research in Mathematics Education* 38, no. 3 (May 2007): 258–88.

- Professional development on bringing in algebraic reasoning to elementary math lessons improved students' grasp of mathematical content. Speaks to potential benefits of using a curriculum that builds in the teaching of algebraic thinking at the elementary level.

Jerrim, John, Luis Alejandro Lopez-Agudo, and Oscar D. Marcenaro-Gutierrez. "Does it matter what children read? New evidence using longitudinal census data from Spain." *Oxford Review of Education* 46, no. 5 (2020): 515–33. https://doi.org/10.1080/03054985.2020.1723516.

- It's widely stated that reading every day is essential for kids' literacy development. This longitudinal study makes the compelling case that this is only the case when students read books and not other printed material.

Johns Hopkins University, School of Education. *School Culture 360™ for face-to-face and remote learning contexts.* Accessed November 16, 2021. https://edpolicy.education.jhu.edu/school-culture/.

Johnson, Evelyn S., and Lisa Boyd. "Designing effective Tier 2 reading instruction in early elementary grades with limited resources." *Intervention in School and Clinic* 48, no. 4 (2013): 203–09. https://doi.org/10.1177%2F1053451212462881.

- Interventions should include knowledge-building activities.

Jordan, Phyllis W. "Nudging students and families to better attendance." *Sound and Fury* (blog), FutureEd, December 22, 2018. https://www.future-ed.org/nudging-students-and-families-to-better-attendance/.

K

Kaefer, Tanya, Susan B. Neuman, and Ashley M. Pinkham. "Pre-existing background knowledge influences socioeconomic differences in preschoolers' word learning and comprehension." *Reading Psychology* 36, no. 3 (2014): 203–31. http://dx.doi.org/10.1080/02702711.2013.843064.

- Students from lower-income backgrounds perform equally well on measures of reading comprehension when explicitly taught relevant background knowledge. This indicates background knowledge's significant role in reading comprehension and points to its potential to reduce the achievement gap.

Karpicke, Jeffrey D. and Janell R. Blunt. "Retrieval practice produces more learning than elaborative studying with concept mapping." *Science* 331, no. 6018 (February 2011): 772–75. https://doi.org/10.1126/science.1199327.

Kaufman, Julia and Rebecca Kockler. *Lessons from Louisiana's efforts to create a new marketplace for high-quality K–12 curricula and professional development.* Washington, DC: American Enterprise Institute, June 2020. https://www.aei.org/research-products/report/lessons-from-louisianas-efforts-to-create-a-new-marketplace-for-high-quality-k-12-curricula-and-professional-development/.

Kaufman, Julia, Lindsey Thompson, and V. Darleen Opfer. *Creating a coherent system to support instruction aligned with State Standards: Promising practices of the Louisiana Department of Education.* Santa Monica, CA: RAND Corporation, 2016. https://www.rand.org/pubs/research_reports/RR1613.html.

- Describes the successes of the Louisiana Department of Education in promoting the use of high-quality (and therefore content-rich) ELA materials.

Keels, Micere, and Tynisha Jointer. *Preparing schools to meet the needs of students coping with trauma and toxic stress.* Brief no. 17, EdResearch for Recovery Project, Results for America, Annenberg Institute for School Reform at Brown University, May 2021. https://annenberg.brown.edu/sites/default/files/EdResearch_for_Recovery_Brief_17.pdf.

Keesor, Carolyn A. "Administrative visibility and its effect on classroom behavior." *NASSP Bulletin* 89, no. 643 (June 2005): 64–73. https://doi.org/10.1177/019263650508964306.

Kennedy, Julie. "Intellectual prep: What we've learned." Charter School Growth Fund, July 13, 2019. https://stories.chartergrowthfund.org/intellectual-prep-what-weve-learned-5ce0506e03f9.

Kidron, Yael, and Jim Lindsay. *The effects of increased learning time on student academic and nonacademic outcomes: Findings from a meta-analytic review.* REL 2014-015. Washington, DC: US Department of Education, Institute of Education Sciences, National Center for Education Evaluation and Regional Assistance, Regional Educational Laboratory Appalachia, July 2014. https://ies.ed.gov/ncee/edlabs/regions/appalachia/pdf/REL_2014015.pdf.

Killion, Joellen. *Assessing impact: Evaluating professional learning.* Thousand Oaks, CA: Corwin and Learning Forward, 2008. https://us.corwin.com/en-us/nam/assessing-impact/book257259.

Kilpatrick, David A. *Essentials of assessing, preventing, and overcoming reading difficulties*, edited by Alan S. Kaufman and Nadeen L. Kaufman. Hoboken, NJ: Wiley, 2015.

- Describes the "three-cueing" system and paints a picture of how pseudoscience can come to take hold in educational practices.

Koedel, Cory and Morgan Polikoff. "Big bang for just a few bucks: The impact of math textbooks in California." *Evidence Speaks Reports – 2*, Brookings Institution, no. 5 (January 5, 2017). https://www.brookings.edu/research/big-bang-for-just-a-few-bucks-the-impact-of-math-textbooks-in-california/.

- Finds that non-trivial gains in student achievement are attainable simply by choosing more effective curriculum materials, with effect sizes on par with what one could expect from a hypothetical policy that substantially increases the quality of the teaching workforce. "Choosing a more effective textbook is a seemingly straightforward policy option for raising student achievement."

Kosanovich, Marcia, Laurie Lee, and Barbara Foorman. *A second grade teacher's guide to supporting family involvement in foundational reading skills*. REL 2021–053. Washington, DC: US Department of Education, Institute of Education Sciences, National Center for Education Evaluation and Regional Assistance, Regional Educational Laboratory Southeast, February 2021. https://ies.ed.gov/ncee/edlabs/regions/southeast/pdf/REL_2021053.pdf.

Kosanovich, Marcia, Laurie Lee, and Barbara Foorman. *A third-grade teacher's guide to supporting family involvement in foundational reading skills*. Washington, DC: US Department of Education, Institute of Education Sciences, National Center for Education Evaluation and Regional Assistance, Regional Educational Laboratory Southeast, April 2021. https://ies.ed.gov/ncee/edlabs/projects/project.asp?projectID=5673.

Kosslyn, Stephen M. "The science of learning: Mechanisms and principles." In *Building the intentional university: Minerva and the future of higher education*, edited by Stephen M. Kosslyn and Ben Nelson, 209–36. Cambridge, MA: MIT Press, 2017.

Kraft, Matthew A. "Teacher effects on complex cognitive skills and social-emotional competencies." *Journal of Human Resources* 54, no. 1 (2019): 1–36. https://scholar.harvard.edu/mkraft/publications/teacher-effects-complex-cognitive-skills-and-social-emotional-competencies.

Kraft, Matthew A. and Grace Falken. *A blueprint for scaling tutoring across public schools*. EdWorkingPaper 20-335. Providence, RI: Annenberg Institute at Brown University, 2021. https://doi.org/10.26300/dkjh-s987.

Kraft, Matthew A., William H. Marinell, and Darrick Shen-Wei Yee. "School organizational contexts, teacher turnover, and student achievement: Evidence from panel data." *American Educational Research Journal* 53, no. 5, October 2016: 1411–49. https://doi.org/10.3102/0002831216667478.

Kroesbergen, Evelyn H., Johannes E. H. Van Luit, and Cora J. M. Maas. "Effectiveness of explicit and constructivist mathematics instruction for low-achieving students in the Netherlands." *The Elementary School Journal* 104, no. 3 (January 2004): 233–51. https://doi.org/10.1086/499751.

Kuhn, Deanna, and Susan Pearsall. "Developmental origins of scientific thinking." *Journal of Cognition and Development* 1, no. 1 (2000): 113–29. https://doi.org/10.1207/S15327647JCD0101N_11.

L

Lake, Robin, and Lynn Olson. *Learning as we go: Principles for effective assessment during the COVID-19 pandemic.* Bothel, WA: Center on Reinventing Public Education, The Evidence Project, 2020. https://crpe.org/wp-content/uploads/final_diagnostics_brief_2020.pdf.

- Cautions against using assessment results "as a gatekeeper to grade-level content or to track students into low-level content, which may increase the achievement gap and historically have been much more likely for English language learners and students of color." Instead, assessment results should identify students' strengths and "build on those strengths while addressing their needs."

Langley, Audra K., Erum Nadeem, Sheryl H. Kataoka, Bradley D. Stein, and Lisa H. Jaycox. "Evidence-based mental health programs in schools: Barriers and facilitators of successful implementation." *School Mental Health* 2 no. 3 (May 2010): 105–13. https://doi.org/10.1007/s12310-010-9038-1.

LaVenia, Mark. *The state of the instructional materials market: 2019 report.* Durham, NC: EdReports, April 3, 2020. https://www.edreports.org/resources/article/2019-state-of-the-market-report.

Learn Well, *Addressing K–12 students' emerging mental health needs: How educators can respond to students' anxiety and stress.* White paper. Plymouth, Massachusetts: Learn Well, December 2020. https://learnwellservices.com/wp-content/uploads/2020/12/LW_K12MentalHealth_WP_FINAL.pdf.

Lemov, Doug. *Teach like a champion 3.0.* Hoboken, NJ: Wiley, 2021.

Lemov, Doug, Erica Woolway, and Katie Yezzi. *Practice perfect.* Hoboken, NJ: Wiley, 2012.

Leonard, James F. *The new philosophy for K-12 education: A Deming framework for transforming America's schools.* Milwaukee, WI: ASQ Quality Press, May 1996.

Louisiana Department of Education. *Curriculum.* Accessed November 16, 2021. https://www.louisianabelieves.com/academics/curriculum.

Louisiana Department of Education. "Instructional materials evaluation review for alignment in science grades K – 12 (IMET)." October 9, 2019. https://www.louisianabelieves.com/docs/default-source/curricular-resources/amplify-education-inc---amplify-science-la-edition-grades-k-5-(-2019).pdf?sfvrsn=58439a1f_4.

Louisiana Department of Education. "Instructional materials evaluation - student standards review." June 24, 2016. https://www.louisianabelieves.com/docs/default-source/curricular-resources/core-knowledge-ckla-ela-grade-3.pdf?sfvrsn=4fe28c1f_10.

M

Manning, Julia, and Lieny Jeon. *Teacher stress and second-hand trauma: Supporting teachers during re-entry.* Baltimore, MD: Johns Hopkins University, Institute for Education Policy, August 2020. http://jhir.library.jhu.edu/handle/1774.2/63228.

Markowitz, Anna J., Daphna Bassok, Amy Smith, and Sarah Kiscaden. *Study of early education in Louisiana COVID-19 survey.* Report No. 2. EdPolicyWorks at University of Virginia, UCLA Graduate School of Education and Information Studies, July 2020. http://www.see-partnerships.com/uploads/1/3/2/8/132824390/seela_covid_teacher_report.pdf.

Mattison, Erica, and Mark S. Aber. "Closing the achievement gap: The association of racial climate with achievement and behavioral outcomes." *American Journal of Community Psychology* 40, no. 1–2 (June 2007): 1–12. https://doi.org/10.1007/s10464-007-9128-x.

Mavrogordato, Madeline, Rebecca Callahan, David DeMatthews, and Elena Izquierdo. "Supports for students who are English learners." Brief no. 15. EdResearch for Recovery Project, Results for America, Annenberg Institute for School Reform at Brown University, February 2021. https://annenberg.brown.edu/sites/default/files/EdResearch_for_Recovery_Brief_15.pdf.

May, Henry, and Marian A. Robinson. "A randomized evaluation of Ohio's Personalized Assessment Reporting System (PARS)." Philadelphia, PA: Consortium for Policy Research in Education, University of Pennsylvania, December 2007. https://repository.upenn.edu/cpre_researchreports/50/.

McDaniel, Mark A., and Ronald P. Fisher. "Tests and test feedback as learning sources." *Contemporary Educational Psychology* 16, no. 2 (1991): 192–201. https://doi.org/10.1016/0361-476X(91)90037-L.

- Tested facts (for which feedback was provided) are better recalled on a final criterion test than untested facts, showing the beneficial effects of testing.

McKeown, Margaret G., Isabel L. Beck, and Ronette G. K. Blake. "Rethinking reading comprehension instruction: A comparison of instruction for strategies and content approaches." *Reading Research Quarterly* 44, no. 3 (2009): 218–53. https://doi.org/10.1598/RRQ.44.3.1.

McNamara, Danielle S., Eileen Kintsch, Nancy Butler Songer, and Walter Kintsch. "Are good texts always better? Interactions of text coherence, background knowledge, and levels of understanding in learning from text." *Cognition and Instruction* 14, no. 1 (1996): 1–43. https://doi.org/10.1207/s1532690xci1401_1.

- Strong background knowledge helps students comprehend texts that are not well written or coherent. This suggests that the type of background knowledge built by history and science lessons is more decisive in reading comprehension than even high-quality texts.

Meadows, Donella. *Thinking in systems: A primer.* White River Junction, VT: Chelsea Green Publishing Company, 2008.

The Meadows Center for Preventing Educational Risk. *10 key policies and practices for reading intervention.* Austin, TX: The Meadows Center for Preventing Educational Risk, University of Texas at Austin, 2000. https://www.meadowscenter.org/files/resources/10Key_ReadingIntervention_WEB-Rev2.pdf.

Metz, Kathleen E. "Narrowing the gulf between the practices of science and the elementary school science classroom." *The Elementary School Journal* 109, no. 2 (January 2008): 138–61. http://dx.doi.org/10.1086/590523.

Minahan, Jessica. "Trauma-informed teaching strategies." *Educational Leadership*, October 1, 2019. http://www.ascd.org/publications/educational_leadership/oct19/vol77/num02/Trauma-Informed_Teaching_Strategies.aspx.

Moats, Louisa Cook. *Whole language lives on: The illusion of "balanced" reading instruction.* Washington DC: Thomas B. Fordham Institute, October 2000. https://eric.ed.gov/?id=ED449465.

- Critiques the whole language and balanced literacy approach to teaching reading, and argues that the science around teaching reading points to systematic phonics instruction.

Morgan, Paul L., George Farkas, and Steve Maczuga. "Which instructional practices most help first-grade students with and without mathematics difficulties?" *Educational Evaluation and Policy Analysis* 37, no. 2 (2015): 184–205. https://doi.org/10.3102/0162373714536608.

Mueller, Pam A., and Daniel M. Oppenheimer. "The pen is mightier than the keyboard: Advantages of longhand over laptop note taking." *Psychological Science* 25, no. 6 (April 2014): 1159–68. https://doi.org/10.1177/0956797614524581.

- Two key takeaways: the benefits of writing for information retention are strongest with writing by hand rather than on the computer; and the act of writing solidifies students' knowledge of a subject.

Muis, Krista R., Cynthia Psaradellis, Marianne Chevrier, Ivana Di Leo, and Susanne P. Lajoie. "Learning by preparing to teach: Fostering self-regulatory processes and achievement during complex mathematics problem solving." *Journal of Educational Psychology* 108, no. 4 (2016): 474–492. http://dx.doi.org/10.1037/edu0000071.

N

Naff, David, Shenita Williams, Jenna Furman, and Melissa Lee. *Supporting student mental health during and after COVID-19.* Richmond, VA: Metropolitan Educational Research Consortium, 2020. https://scholarscompass.vcu.edu/cgi/viewcontent.cgi?article=1111&context=merc_pubs.

Nagaoka, Jenny, Camille Farrington, Stacy B. Ehrlich, Ryan D. Heath, David W. Johnson, Sarah Dickson, Ashley Cureton Turner, Ashley Mayo, and Kathleen Hayes. *Foundations for young adult success: A developmental framework.* CCSR concept paper. UChicago Consortium on Research, Chicago, Illinois, June 2015. https://consortium.uchicago.edu/publications/foundations-young-adult-success-developmental-framework.

Naka, Makiko and Hiroshi Naoi. "The effect of repeated writing on memory." *Memory & Cognition* 23, no. 2 (1995): 201–12. https://psycnet.apa.org/doi/10.3758/BF03197222.

- Demonstrates the crucial link between writing about something and remembering the content involved.

National Center for Learning Disabilities. *Promising practices to accelerate learning for students with disabilities during COVID-19 and beyond.* Washington, DC: National Center for Learning Disabilities, 2021. https://www.ncld.org/wp-content/uploads/2021/02/2021-NCLD-Promising-Practices-to-Accelerate-Learning_FINAL.pdf.

National Center on Education and the Economy (NCEE). *Top performing countries.* Accessed November 22, 2021. https://ncee.org/top-performing-countries/.

National Center on Safe Supportive Learning Environments. *Trauma-sensitive schools training package.* Washington, DC: National Center on Safe Supportive Learning Environments, American Institutes for Research, 2018. https://safesupportivelearning.ed.gov/trauma-sensitive-schools-training-package.

National Council of Teachers of Mathematics (NCTM), National Council of Supervisors of Mathematics (NCSM), "Moving forward: Mathematics learning in the era of COVID-19." June 2020. https://www.nctm.org/uploadedFiles/Research_and_Advocacy/NCTM_NCSM_Moving_Forward.pdf.

- NCTM encourages grade-level teams to work, with the support of district leaders, to identify essential learning and focus on the major work of each grade. It points to the Mathematics Coherence Map by Student Achievement Partners to identify prerequisite understandings that can help target supports to students with gaps.

National Reading Panel. *Teaching children to read: An evidence-based assessment of the scientific research literature on reading and its implications for reading instruction.* Washington, DC: US Department of Health and Human Services, National Institutes of Health, National Institute of Child Health and Human Development, National Reading Panel, April 2000. https://www.nichd.nih.gov/sites/default/files/publications/pubs/nrp/Documents/report.pdf.

National Research Council. *How people learn: Brain, mind, experience, and school: Expanded edition.* Washington, DC: The National Academies Press, 2000. https://doi.org/10.17226/9853.

National Research Council. *Taking science to school: Learning and teaching science in grades K-8,* edited by Richard A. Duschl, Heidi A. Schweingruber, and Andrew W. Shouse. Washington, DC: The National Academies Press, 2007.

National School Climate Center. "What is school climate and why is it important?" Accessed November 16, 2021. https://www.schoolclimate.org/school-climate.

National Scientific Council on the Developing Child. *Supportive relationships and active skill-building strengthen the foundations of resilience.* Working Paper 13. Cambridge, MA: National Scientific Council on the Developing Child, Center on the Developing Child at Harvard University, 2015. https://46y5eh11fhgw3ve3ytpwxt9r-wpengine.netdna-ssl.com/wp-content/uploads/2015/05/The-Science-of-Resilience2.pdf.

National Student Support Accelerator. "High-impact tutoring." Accessed November 19, 2021. https://studentsupportaccelerator.com/about/high-impact-tutoring.

Nelson, Barbara Scott, and James K. Hammerman. "Reconceptualizing teaching: Moving toward the creation of intellectual communities of students, teachers and teacher educators." In *Teacher learning: New policies, new practices. The Series on School Reform,* edited by Milbrey McLaughlin and Ida Oberman. Newton, MA: Teacher College Press,1996.

- Provides a framework for the idea of classrooms as "intellectual communities" that are the ultimate end of the rules and relationships that foster positive behavior.

Nestojko, John F., Dung C. Bui, Nate Kornell and Elizabeth Ligon Bjork. "Expecting to teach enhances learning and organization of knowledge in free recall of text passages." *Memory & Cognition* no. 42 (2014): 1038–48. https://doi.org/10.3758/s13421-014-0416-z.

Neuman, Susan, Tanya Kaefer, Ashley Pinkham. "Building background knowledge." *Reading Rockets.* Accessed November 18, 2021. https://www.readingrockets.org/article/building-background-knowledge.

Ng, Swee Fong, and Kerry Lee. "The Model Method: Singapore children's tool for representing and solving algebraic word problems. *Journal for Research in Mathematics Education* 40, no. 3 (2009): 282–313. https://www.jstor.org/stable/40539338.

- The method of model drawing used in Singapore's national math curriculum for nearly all word problems has had a positive impact on student achievement.

Nichols-Barrer, Ira and Joshua Haimson. *Impacts of five expeditionary learning middle schools on academic achievement.* Cambridge, MA: Mathematica, July 8, 2013. https://www.mathematica.org/our-publications-and-findings/publications/impacts-of-five-expeditionary-learning-middle-schools-on-academic-achievement.

- Mathematica found stronger academic results in ELA (and also math) for schools using EL Education's (then called Expeditionary Learning) curricula.

Nickow, Andre, Philip Oreopoulos, and Vincent Quan. *The impressive effects of tutoring on preK-12 learning: A systematic review and meta-analysis of the experimental evidence.* NBER Working Paper 27476. Cambridge, MA: NBER, July 2020. https://doi.org/10.3386/w27476.

Norris, Tori Kim. *Elaborative rehearsal: An examination of usage, perceptions of utility, and differences in metacognition and test performance.* PhD diss., University of South Carolina, 2019. https://scholarcommons.sc.edu/etd/5474/.

O

O'Conner, Rosemarie, Jessica De Feyter, Alyssa Carr, Jia Lisa Luo, and Helen Romm. *A review of the literature on social and emotional learning for students ages 3-8: Outcomes for different student populations and settings (Part 4 of 4).* REL 2017-248. Washington, DC: US Department of Education, Institute of Education Sciences, National Center for Education Evaluation and Regional Assistance, Regional Educational Laboratory Mid-Atlantic, February 2017. https://eric.ed.gov/?id=ED572724.

- SEL programs seem to have a bigger positive impact on students from low-income backgrounds. Only high-quality SEL approaches appear beneficial.

Oliver, Regina, Joseph Wehby, and Daniel Reschly. "Teacher classroom management practices: Effects on disruptive or aggressive student behavior." *Campbell Systematic Reviews* 7, no. 1 (2011): 1–55. http://dx.doi.org/10.4073/csr.2011.4.

- Summary showing how strong classroom management systems based on clear and transparent rules can reduce disruptive student behavior.

Onda, Masayuki, and Edward Seyler. "English learners reclassification and academic achievement: Evidence from Minnesota." *Economics of Education Review* 79 (December 2020). https://doi.org/10.1016/j.econedurev.2020.102043.

Organisation for Economic Cooperation and Development (OECD). "Growth mindset." *In PISA 2018 Results (Volume III): What school life means for students' lives.* Paris: OECD Publishing, 2020. https://doi.org/10.1787/bd69f805-en.

Osterman, Karen F. "Students' need for belonging in the school community." *Review of Educational Research* 70, no. 3 (September 2000): 323–67. https://doi.org/10.3102/00346543070003323.

P

Pan, Steven C. "The interleaving effect: Mixing it up boosts learning." *Mind and Brain* (blog), *Scientific American*, August 4, 2015. https://www.scientificamerican.com/article/the-interleaving-effect-mixing-it-up-boosts-learning/.

Panero, Nell Scharff. "Progressive mastery through deliberate practice: A promising approach for improving writing." *Improving Schools* 19, no. 3 (November 2016): 229–45. https://doi.org/10.1177/1365480216643209.

- Summarizes the research on improving writing quality as well as writing strategies that improve reading comprehension, and connects those to practices taught in *The Writing Revolution*.

Papageorge, Nicholas W., Seth Gershenson, and Kyung Min Kang. "Teacher expectations matter." *The Review of Economics and Statistics* 102, no. 2 (May 2020): 234–51. https://doi.org/10.1162/rest_a_00838.

Pashler, Harold. *Organizing instruction and study to improve student learning: A practice guide.* NCER 2007-2004. Washington, DC: US Department of Education, Institute of Education Sciences, National Center for Education Research, 2007. https://ies.ed.gov/ncee/wwc/PracticeGuide/1.

Pikulski, John J. and David J. Chard. "Fluency: Bridge between decoding and reading comprehension." *The Reading Teacher* 58, no. 6 (November 2011): 510–19. https://doi.org/10.1598/RT.58.6.2.

Pimentel, Susan. "Expanding the important national conversation about reading." Thomas B. Fordham Institute, November 8, 2011. https://fordhaminstitute.org/national/commentary/expanding-important-national-conversation-about-reading.

Pimentel, Susan. "Why doesn't every teacher know the research on reading instruction?" *Education Week*, October 26, 2018. https://www.edweek.org/teaching-learning/opinion-why-doesnt-every-teacher-know-the-research-on-reading-instruction/2018/10.

- Outlines the crucial role that building content knowledge plays in building literacy.

Polikoff, Morgan and Jennifer Dean. *The supplemental curriculum bazaar: Is what's online any good?* Washington DC: Thomas B. Fordham Institute, December 2019. https://fordhaminstitute.org/national/research/supplemental-curriculum-bazaar.

Polikoff, Morgan, Elaine Wang, Shira Haderlein, Julia Kaufman, Ashley Woo, Daniel Silver, and V. Opfer. *Exploring coherence in English language arts instructional systems in the Common Core era.* Santa Monica, CA: RAND Corporation, 2020. https://doi.org/10.7249/RRA279-1.

- Describes more ways in which non-evidence-backed ideas about teaching reading can have damaging effects.

Pomerance, Laura, Julie Greenberg, and Kate Walsh. "Learning about learning: What every new teacher needs to know." Washington, DC: National Council on Teacher Quality, 2016. https://www.nctq.org/dmsView/Learning_About_Learning_Report.

Pondiscio, Robert. *How the other half learns: Equality, excellence, and the battle over school choice.* New York, NY: Avery, 2019.

- Points to the important role of being transparent and direct with parents, among other successful aspects of Success Academies Charter Schools.

Pounds, Jessie. "Teaching the teachers: Guilford runs its own licensure program." *News and Record* (NC), February 5, 2017. https://greensboro.com/blogs/the_chalkboard/teaching-the-teachers-guilford-runs-its-own-licensure-program/article_1d43dc0e-ebd1-5d9e-8958-8441332c8a01.html.

Q

Quin, Daniel. "Longitudinal and contextual associations between teacher–student relationships and student engagement: A systematic review." *Review of Educational Research* 87, no. 2 (April 2017): 345–87. https://www.jstor.org/stable/44667659.

- Review of 46 studies on the impact of strong relationships between teachers and students that decisively shows positive impacts on academics, attendance, positive behavior, and many other areas.

Quinn, David M. "Experimental evidence on teachers' racial bias in student evaluation: The role of grading scales." *Educational Evaluation and Policy Analysis* 42, no. 3 (September 2020): 375–92. https://doi.org/10.3102/0162373720932188.

R

Rasinski, Timothy V. "Readers who struggle: Why many struggle and a modest proposal for improving their reading." *The Reading Teacher* 70, no. 5 (March/April 2017): 519–24. https://doi.org/10.1002/trtr.1533.

Rauch, Jonathan. *The constitution of knowledge: A defense of truth.* Washington DC: Brookings Institution Press, June 2021.

Raviv, Tali, Christopher M. Warren, Jason J. Washburn, Madeleine K. Kanaley, Liga Eihentale, Hayley Jane Goldenthal, Jaclyn Russo, et al. "Caregiver perceptions of children's psychological well-being during the COVID-19 pandemic." *JAMA Network Open* 4, no. 4 (April 2021). https://doi.org/10.1001/jamanetworkopen.2021.11103.

Recht, Donna R. and Lauren Leslie. "Effect of prior knowledge on good and poor readers' memory of text." *Journal of Educational Psychology* 80, no.1 (1988): 16–20. https://doi.org/10.1037/0022-0663.80.1.16.

Reeves, Douglas and Rick DuFour. "The futility of PLC lite." *Phi Delta Kappan*, March 1, 2016. https://kappanonline.org/the-futility-of-plc-lite/.

Riddle, Travis, and Stacey Sinclair. "Racial disparities in school-based disciplinary actions are associated with county-level rates of racial bias." *PNAS* 116, no. 17 (April 2019): 8255–60. https://doi.org/10.1073/pnas.1808307116.

Rittle-Johnson, Bethany, Jon R. Star, and Kelley Durkin. "The importance of prior knowledge when comparing examples: Influences on conceptual and procedural knowledge of equation solving." *Journal of Educational Psychology* 101, no. 4 (2009): 836–52. https://doi.org/10.1037/a0016026.

- Students' prior conceptual and procedural knowledge is essential at the elementary school level and even more important in middle-school algebra classes.

Roberts, Greg, Nancy Scammacca, David J. Osman, Colby Hall, Sarojani S. Mohammed, and Sharon Vaughn. "Team-based learning: Moderating effects of metacognitive elaborative rehearsal and middle school history content recall." *Educational Psychology Review* 26, no. 3 (2014): 451–68. http://www.jstor.org/stable/43548435.

Rohrer, Doug, and Kelli Taylor. "The effects of overlearning and distributed practice on the retention of mathematics knowledge." *Applied Cognitive Psychology* 20 (2006): 1209–24. https://files.eric.ed.gov/fulltext/ED505642.pdf.

Rollins, Suzy Pepper. *Learning in the fast lane: 8 ways to put ALL students on the road to academic success*. Alexandria, VA: Association for Supervision and Curriculum Development (ASCD), April 2014.

Romer, Natalie, Nathaniel von der Embse, Katie Eklund, Stephen Kilgus, Kelly Perales, Joni Williams Splett, Shannon Suldo, and David Wheeler. *Best practices in universal social, emotional, and behavioral screening: An implementation guide*. Version 2.0. Madison, WI: School Mental Health Collaborative, 2020. https://smhcollaborative.org/wp-content/uploads/2019/11/universalscreening.pdf.

Romero, Mariajosé, and Young-Sun Lee. *A national portrait of chronic absenteeism in the early grades*. New York, NY: National Center for Children in Poverty, Columbia University, October 2007. https://doi.org/10.7916/D89C7650.

- Confirms the detrimental effects of chronic absenteeism in elementary school on school success by examining children from across various incomes and race/ethnicity groups in a nationally representative sample of children entering kindergarten.

Roorda, Debora L., Helma M. Y. Koomen, Jantine L. Spilt, and Frans J. Oort. "The influence of affective teacher–student relationships on students' school engagement and achievement: A meta-analytic approach." *Review of Educational Research* 81, no. 4 (December 2011): 493–529. https://doi.org/10.3102/0034654311421793.

- Looks across 99 studies to investigate the associations between affective qualities of teacher–student relationships and students' school engagement and achievement to find evidence of the major impact of positive relationships on academic success.

Rosenshine, Barak. *Principles of instruction*. Educational Practices Series–21. Geneva, Switzerland: International Academy of Education, International Bureau of Education, 2010. http://www.ibe.unesco.org/fileadmin/user_upload/Publications/Educational_Practices/EdPractices_21.pdf.

S

Same, Michelle R., Nicole I. Guarino, Max Pardo, Deaweh Benson, Kyle Fagan, and Jim Lindsay. *Evidence-supported interventions associated with Black students' education outcomes: Findings from a systematic review of research*. Washington, DC: US Department of Education, Institute of Education Sciences, Regional Educational Laboratory Midwest, February 2018. http://files.eric.ed.gov/fulltext/ED581117.pdf.

- There is promising evidence for the role that high expectations play in all students' academic outcomes, and particularly so for African-American students.

Santos, Maria, Linda Darling-Hammond, and Tina Cheuk. "Teacher development to support English language learners in the context of Common Core State Standards." Presented at the Understanding Language Conference, January 2012. http://educationdocbox.com/Homework_and_Study_Tips/65981810-Teacher-development-to-support-english-language-learners-in-the-context-of-common-core-state-standards.html#download_tab_content.

Saunders, William M., Claude N. Goldenberg, and Ronald Gallimore. "Increasing achievement by focusing grade-level teams on improving classroom learning: A prospective, quasi-experimental study of title 1 schools." *American Educational Research Journal* 46, no. 4, (2009): 1006–33. https://doi.org/10.3102%2F0002831209333185.

Savitz-Romer, Mandy, Joie Jager-Hyman, and Ann Coles. *Removing roadblocks to rigor: Linking academic and social supports to ensure college readiness and success.* Washington, DC: Pathways to College Network, Institute for Higher Education Policy, April 2009. http://files.eric.ed.gov/fulltext/ED509545.pdf.

Sawchuk, Stephen. "High-dosage tutoring is effective, but expensive. Ideas for making it work." *Education Week*, August 19, 2020. https://www.edweek.org/leadership/high-dosage-tutoring-is-effective-but-expensive-ideas-for-making-it-work/2020/08.

Sawchuk, Stephen. "Students lost time and learning in the pandemic. What 'acceleration' can do to help." *Education Week*, August 19, 2020. https://www.edweek.org/leadership/students-lost-time-and-learning-in-the-pandemic-what-acceleration-can-do-to-help/2020/08.

Schmidt, William, and Curtis McKnight. *Inequality for all: The challenge of unequal opportunity in American schools.* New York, NY: Teachers College Press, 2012.

Schneider, Barbara. "Trust in schools: A core resource for school reform." *Educational Leadership*, March 1, 2003. http://www.ascd.org/publications/educational-leadership/mar03/vol60/num06/Trust-in-Schools@-A-Core-Resource-for-School-Reform.aspx.

Scholtes, Peter R. *The leader's handbook: Making things happen, getting things done.* New York, NY: McGraw-Hill, 1997. https://pscholtes.com/handbook.htm.

Schueler, Beth and Martin West. *'It was not like a normal summer school at all': The National Summer School Initiative implementation study.* EdPolicyWorks Reports Series No 9, University of Virginia, Charlottesville, VA, December 2020. https://curry.virginia.edu/sites/default/files/uploads/epw/NSSI%20Brief_12.05.2020%20merged_0.pdf.

Search Institute. "The Developmental Relationships Framework," Minneapolis, MN, 2020. https://www.search-institute.org/developmental-relationships/developmental-relationships-framework/.

Sebring, Penny Bender, Elaine Allensworth, Anthony S. Bryk, John Q. Easton, and Stuart Luppescu. *The essential supports for school improvement.* Chicago, IL: UChicago Consortium on School Research, September 2006. https://consortium.uchicago.edu/publications/essential-supports-school-improvement.

Seider, Scott. *Character compass: How powerful school culture can point students toward success.* Cambridge, MA: Harvard Education Press, 2012. https://www.hepg.org/hep-home/books/character-compass_169.

Seven, Sabriye, Asiye Pinar Koksal, and Gulsen Kocak. "The effect of carrying out writing to learn activities on academic success of fifth grade students in secondary school on the subject of 'force and motion'." *Universal Journal of Educational Research* 5, no. 5 (2017): 744–49. https://doi.org/10.13189/ujer.2017.050506.

Shafer, Leah. "What makes a good school culture?" Harvard University: Graduate School of Education, July 23, 2018. https://www.gse.harvard.edu/news/uk/18/07/what-makes-good-school-culture.

Shanahan, Timothy. "New evidence on teaching reading at frustration levels." Shanahan on Literacy (blog), May 28, 2017. https://www.readingrockets.org/blogs/shanahan-literacy/new-evidence-teaching-reading-frustration-levels.

- Students make more progress in reading achievement when they read texts that are considered to be above their grade level.

Shanahan, Timothy. "Why children should be taught to read with more challenging texts." *Perspectives on Language*, Fall 2019. http://digitaleditions.sheridan.com/publication/?i=644729&article_id=3571279&view=articleBrowser&ver=html5.

- Debunks the research on the incorrect idea that children should be taught to read with leveled readers.

Sharkey, Patrick. "The acute effect of local homicides on children's cognitive performance." *PNAS* 107, no. 26 (June 2010): 11733–38. https://doi.org/10.1073/pnas.1000690107.

Shaywitz, Sally, and Jonathan Shawywitz. "Overcoming dyslexia: A new and complete science-based program for reading problems at any level." *Alfred A. Knopf* (blog) n. d. Accessed November 23, 2021. http://knopfdoubleday.com/2020/03/03/overcoming-dyslexia-by-sally-shaywitz-md-and-jonathan-shaywitz-md/.

Sheldon, Steven B. "Improving student attendance with school, family, and community partnerships." *Journal of Educational Research* 100, no. 5 (May–June 2007): 267–75. https://doi.org/10.3200/JOER.100.5.267-275.

- A robust family engagement strategy plays a key role in improving attendance.

Short, Jim and Stephanie Hirsh. *The elements: Transforming teaching through curriculum-based professional learning*. Pittsburgh, PA: Carnegie, November 2020. https://www.carnegie.org/topics/topic-articles/professional-learning-educators/elements-transforming-teaching-through-curriculum-based-professional-learning/.

Siegler, Robert, Thomas Carpenter, Francis Fennell, David Geary, James Lewis, Yukari Okamoto, Laurie Thompson, and Jonathan Wray. *Developing effective fractions instruction for kindergarten through 8th grade: A practice guide*. NCEE 2010-4039. Washington, DC: National Center for Education Evaluation and Regional Assistance, Institute of Education Sciences, US Department of Education, September 2010. https://ies.ed.gov/ncee/wwc/PracticeGuide/15.

Simmons, Dena. "Why we can't afford whitewashed social-emotional learning." *Educational Leadership* (blog), April 1, 2019. https://www.ascd.org/el/articles/why-we-cant-afford-whitewashed-social-emotional-learning.

Simonsen, Brandi, Sarah Fairbanks, Amy Briesch, Diane Myers, and George Sugai. "Evidence-based practices in classroom management: Considerations for research to practice." *Education and Treatment of Children* 31, no. 3 (2008): 351–80. https://eric.ed.gov/?id=EJ798223.

- Summary of research that finds evidence that setting and reinforcing clear expectations for behavior is an effective classroom-management practice.

Skinner, Ellen, and Michael J. Belmont. "Motivation in the classroom: Reciprocal effects of teacher behavior and student engagement across the school year." *Journal of Educational Psychology* 85, no. 4 (1993): 571–81. https://doi.org/10.1037/0022-0663.85.4.571.

Sklad, Marcin, René Diekstra, Monique De Ritter, Jehonathan Ben, and Carolien Gravesteijn. "Effectiveness of school-based universal social, emotional, and behavioral programs: Do they enhance students' development in the area of skill, behavior, and adjustment?" *Psychology in the Schools* 49, no. 9 (2012): 892–909. https://doi.org/10.1002/pits.21641.

- Meta-analysis of 70 studies points to the positive impact of SEL on "social skills, antisocial behavior, substance abuse, positive self-image, academic achievement, mental health, and prosocial behavior."

Slavin, Robert. "New findings on tutoring: Four shockers." *Robert Slavin's Blog*, April 5, 2018. https://robertslavinsblog.wordpress.com/2018/04/05/new-findings-on-tutoring-four-shockers/.

- One finding is that tutoring by paraprofessionals was at least as effective as tutoring by teachers. Slavin postulates that among the reasons tutoring works is that, in addition to individualization, it provides nurturing and attention.

Somma, Victoria. *The impact of lesson study on teacher effectiveness*. PhD diss., St. John's University, 2016. https://eric.ed.gov/?id=ED577915.

Sparks, Sarah D. "Triaging for trauma during COVID-19." *Education Week*, September 2, 2020. https://www.edweek.org/leadership/triaging-for-trauma-during-covid-19/2020/09.

Stanovich, Keith E. "Matthew effects in reading: Some consequences of individual differences in the acquisition of literacy." *Reading Research Quarterly* 22, no. 4 (Fall 1986): 360–407. https://www.psychologytoday.com/files/u81/Stanovich__1986_.pdf.

- Spells out the impact of the Matthew Effect on literacy acquisition. There are big implications for students' long-term ELA achievement based on how much knowledge is or is not taught throughout their education.

Steiner, David. *Curriculum research: What we know and where we need to go*. StandardsWork, 2017. https://standardswork.org/wp-content/uploads/2017/03/sw-curriculum-research-report-fnl.pdf.

- Research indicates that curriculum is a critical factor in student academic success, particularly in the upper grades, and that comprehensive, content-rich curriculum is a common feature of academically high-performing countries.

Stemler, Steven, Damian Bebell, and Lauren Ann Sonnabend. "Using school mission statements for reflection and research." *Educational Administration Quarterly* 47, no. 2 (November 2011): 383–420. https://doi.org/10.1177%2F0013161X10387590.

Stiegler, Kerri, and Nancy Lever. "Summary of recognized evidence-based programs implemented by Expanded School Mental Health (ESMH) programs." Center for School Mental Health, University of Maryland School of Medicine, 2008. https://safesupportivelearning.ed.gov/sites/default/files/sssta/20110322_EBPMatrix6.08.pdf.

Stiggins, Rick. "Assessment through the student's eyes." *Educational Leadership* 64, no. 8 (2007): 22–6. https://pdo.ascd.org/lmscourses/PD11OC106/media/USM_M6_Reading_Students_Eyes.pdf.

Student Achievement Partners. *Priority instructional content in English language arts/literacy and mathematics*. New York, NY: Student Achievement Partners, June 2020. https://achievethecore.org/page/3267/priority-instructional-content-in-english-language-arts-literacy-and-mathematics.

Student Achievement Partners. *K-8 publishers' criteria for the Common Core State Standards for mathematics*, New York, NY: Student Achievement Partners, 2013. https://achievethecore.org/content/upload/Math_Publishers_Criteria_K-8_Spring_2013_FINAL.pdf.

- The basis for the quality indicators used by EdReports in its curriculum reviews. Describes necessary instructional shifts and establishes criteria for how those should show up in curriculum.

Substance Abuse and Mental Health Services Administration. *SAMHSA's concept of trauma and guidance for a trauma-informed approach.* HHS Publication No. (SMA) 14-4884. Rockville, MD: Substance Abuse and Mental Health Services Administration, June 2014. https://ncsacw.samhsa.gov/userfiles/files/SAMHSA_Trauma.pdf.

Substance Abuse and Mental Health Services Administration, "Trauma and violence." Accessed November 18, 2021. https://www.samhsa.gov/trauma-violence.

T

Tajika, Hidetsugu, Narao Nakatsu, Hironari Nozaki, Ewald Neumann, and Shunichi Maruno. "Effects of self-explanation as a metacognitive strategy for solving mathematical word problems." *Japanese Psychological Research* 49, no. 3 (2007): 222–33. https://doi.org/10.1111/j.1468-5884.2007.00349.x.

- Promoting students' ability to explain their thinking has a positive impact on their ability to solve math word problems.

Takahashi, Akihiko, and Thomas McDougal. "Collaborative lesson research: Maximizing the impact of lesson study." *ZDM* no. 48 (2016): 513–26. https://doi.org/10.1007/s11858-015-0752-x.

- Looks at some cases of where Japanese lesson study went wrong and right in the US, recommends a more "America-friendly" version called Collaborative Lesson Research, and presents details and preliminary results from a three-phase model of school-based CLR at 15 urban US schools.

Taylor, Joseph A., Stephen R. Getty, Susan M. Kowalski, Christopher D. Wilson, Janet Carlson, and Pamela Van Scotter. "An efficacy trial of research-based curriculum materials with curriculum-based professional development." *American Educational Research Journal* 52, no. 5 (2015): 984–1017. https://doi.org/10.3102/0002831215585962.

- Highly effective professional learning positions teachers to further their expertise in content knowledge, pedagogical knowledge, and pedagogical content knowledge.

Taylor, Rebecca D., Eva Oberle, Joseph A. Durlak, and Roger P. Weissberg. "Promoting positive youth development through school-based social and emotional learning interventions: A meta-analysis of follow-up effects." *Child Development* 88, no. 4 (2017):1156–71. https://doi.org/10.1111/cdev.12864.

Thompson, Charles, and John S. Zeuli. "The frame and the tapestry: Standards-based reform and professional development." In *Teaching as the learning profession: Handbook of policy and practice*, edited by Darling-Hammond, Linda and Gary Sykes. San Francisco, CA: Jossey-Bass, 1999.

- Learning to teach in new ways requires teachers to examine their current assumptions and beliefs about content, how they teach that content, and how their students learn best.

Tikasz, Diana. "Pause-Reset-Nourish (PRN)* to promote wellbeing: Use as needed to care for your wellness!" Los Angeles, CA: National Child Traumatic Stress Network (NCTS), 2020. https://www.nctsn.org/sites/default/files/resources/fact-sheet/wellbeing-and-wellness.pdf.

Timmermans, Anneke, and Christine Rubie-Davies. "Do teachers differ in the level of expectations or in the extent to which they differentiate in expectations? Relations between teacher-level expectations, teacher background and beliefs, and subsequent student performance." *Educational Research and Evaluation* 24, nos. 3-5 (2018): 241–263. https://doi.org/10.1080/13803611.2018.1550837.

- When teachers hold differentiated expectations for students in their classrooms, this can be related to lower academic achievement. This speaks to the need to norm all teachers on a culture of high expectations before the school year even starts.

Tindle, Richard and Mitchell G. Longstaff. "Writing, reading and listening differentially overload working memory performance across the serial position curve." *Advances in Cognitive Psychology* 11, no. 4 (2015): 147–155. https://dx.doi.org/ 10.5709/acp-0179-6.

The New Teacher Project (TNTP). "The opportunity myth: What students can show us about how school is letting them down—and how to fix it." September 25, 2018. https://tntp.org/assets/documents/TNTP_The-Opportunity-Myth_Web.pdf.

- Finds a larger effect size for adult expectations than other major factors, with the most pronounced impacts on students of color or from low-income families.

The New Teacher Project (TNTP). "COVID-19 school response toolkit." Accessed on November 18, 2021. https://tntp.org/covid-19-school-response-toolkit/view/learning-acceleration-guide.

The New Teacher Project (TNTP) and Zearn. *Accelerate, don't remediate: New evidence from elementary math classrooms.* New York, NY: TNTP, May 2021. https://tntp.org/publications/view/teacher-training-and-classroom-practice/accelerate-dont-remediate.

Trinidad, Jose E. "Collective expectations protecting and preventing academic achievement." *Education & Urban Society* 51, no. 9 (2019): 1147–71. https://doi.org/10.1177/0013124518785444.

- All adults in a school holding high expectations for students is correlated with positive academic outcomes.

Tyner, Adam, and Sarah Kabourek. "How social studies improves elementary literacy." *Social Education* 85, no. 1 (2021): 32–9. https://www.socialstudies.org/sites/default/files/view-article-2021-02/se-85012132.pdf.

Tyner, Adam, and Sarah Kabourek. "Social studies instruction and reading comprehension: Evidence from the early childhood longitudinal study." Washington, DC: Thomas B. Fordham Institute, 2020. https://fordhaminstitute.org/national/resources/social-studies-instruction-and-reading-comprehension.

- A massive federal database of how much instructional time is spent on different subjects reveals that more time on social studies, not English language arts, is associated with improved reading ability.

U

Uchida, Akitoshi, Robert Michael, and Kazuo Mori. "An induced successful performance enhances student self-efficacy and boosts academic achievement." *AERA Open* 4, no. 4 (2018): 1–9. https://doi.org/10.1177/2332858418806198.

- If students believe that they can do something, they experience more academic success.

UDL Guidelines. "The UDL Guidelines." Accessed November 18, 2021. https://udlguidelines.cast.org/.

Uphoff, Norman. "Understanding social capital: Learning from the analysis and experience of participation." In *Social capital: A multifaceted perspective*, edited by Partha Dasgupta and Ismail Serageldin, 215–49. Ithaca, NY: Cornell University Press, 2001.

US Department of Education, Institute of Education Sciences, National Center for Education Evaluation and Regional Assistance. "Practice guides." Accessed November 18, 2021. https://ies.ed.gov/ncee/wwc/PracticeGuides.

US Department of Education, Institute for Education Sciences, Regional Educational Laboratory Program. "Helping young English learners at home: Simple and fun activities to strengthen language development." February 3, 2021. https://ies.ed.gov/ncee/edlabs/regions/west/Events/Details/369.

US Department of Education, Institute for Education Sciences, Regional Educational Laboratory Program. "Supporting young English learners at home." Accessed November 18, 2021. https://ies.ed.gov/ncee/edlabs/regions/west/Resources/CaregiverActivities.

US Department of Education, Institute of Education Sciences, Regional Educational Laboratory West. "Family and caregiver activity to support young math learners' understanding of fractions." November 2020. https://ies.ed.gov/ncee/edlabs/regions/west/Publications/Details/288.

V

Vescio, Vicki, Dorene Ross, and Alyson Adams. "A review of research on the impact of professional learning communities on teaching practice and student learning." *Teaching and Teacher Education: An International Journal of Research and Studies* 24, no. 1 (2008): 80–91. https://doi.org/10.1016/j.tate.2007.01.004.

- A review of research; the collective results suggest that well-developed PLCs have positive impacts on both teaching practice and student achievement.

Voight, Adam. *The racial school-climate gap.* A report from the Region IX Equity Assistance Center at WestEd. San Francisco, CA: WestEd. https://files.eric.ed.gov/fulltext/ED580366.pdf.

W

Watkins, Natasha D., and Mark S. Aber. "Exploring the relationships among race, class, gender, and middle school students' perceptions of school racial climate." *Equity and Excellence in Education* 42, no. 4 (November 2009): 395–411. https://doi.org/10.1080/10665680903260218.

WestEd. "COVID-19 resources for educators: English learners." Accessed November 24, 2021. https://www.wested.org/covid-19-resources/#english-learners for examples.

Wexler, Natalie. *The knowledge gap: The hidden cause of America's broken education system—and how to fix it.* New York, NY: Avery, 2019.

Wexler, Natalie. "Writing and cognitive load theory." *researchED*, June 24, 2019. https://researched.org.uk/2019/06/24/writing-and-cognitive-load-theory/.

- "Writing can impose such a heavy burden on working memory that students become overwhelmed, unable either to improve their writing skill or to benefit from the positive effects that writing can have on reading comprehension and learning in general."

Whitehurst, Grover. *Don't forget curriculum.* Washington, DC: Brookings Institution, October 2009. https://www.brookings.edu/wp-content/uploads/2016/06/1014_curriculum_whitehurst.pdf.

Wiener, Ross, and Susan Pimentel. *Practice what you teach: Connecting curriculum & professional learning in schools.* Washington DC: Aspen Institute, April 2017. https://www.aspeninstitute.org/wp-content/uploads/2017/04/Practice-What-You-Teach.pdf.

Wigelsworth, Michael, Ann Lendrum, Jeremy Oldfield, A. Scott, Isabel Ten Bokkel, Kyrah Tate, and C. Emery. "The impact of trial stage, developer involvement and international transferability on universal social and emotional learning programme outcomes: A meta-analysis." *Cambridge Journal of Education* 46, no. 3 (2016): 347–76. https://doi.org/10.1080/0305764X.2016.1195791.

- International meta-analysis identified a positive impact of SEL interventions on academic and behavioral outcomes.

Willems, Iris, and Piet Van den Bossche. "Lesson Study effectiveness for teachers' professional learning: a best evidence synthesis." *International Journal for Lesson and Learning Studies* 8, no. 4 (2019): 257–71. http://dx.doi.org/10.1108/IJLLS-04-2019-0031.

- Review of research describing Lesson Study as a powerful professional development approach as a result of its positive impact on teachers' professional learning in terms of knowledge, skills, behavior, and beliefs.

Wiliam, Dylan. "Professional development materials." Accessed November 18, 2021. https://www.dylanwiliam.org/Dylan_Wiliams_website/PD_materials.html.

Willingham, Daniel. "Critical thinking: Why is it so hard to teach?" *American Educator* 31, no. 3 (2007): 8–19. https://www.aft.org/sites/default/files/periodicals/Crit_Thinking.pdf.

Willingham, Daniel. "How knowledge helps." *American Educator* 30, no. 1 (Spring 2006). https://www.aft.org/periodical/american-educator/spring-2006/how-knowledge-helps.

Willingham, Daniel. "Students remember … what they think about." *American Educator* 27, no. 2 (Summer 2003): 37–41. https://www.aft.org/periodical/american-educator/summer-2003/ask-cognitive-scientist-students-rememberwhat.

- Writing can facilitate students' thinking about what they are supposed to learn.

Willingham, Daniel. "The usefulness of brief instruction in reading comprehension strategies." *American Educator* (Winter 2006–07). https://www.aft.org/sites/default/files/periodicals/CogSci.pdf.

- Teaching reading comprehension strategies can be effective for literacy skills if they are taught briefly, with diminishing achievement returns for curricula that overplay their importance.

Willingham, Daniel. "What is developmentally appropriate practice?" *American Educator* 32, no. 3 (2008). https://www.aft.org/sites/default/files/periodicals/willingham_1.pdf.

Willingham, Daniel. *Why don't students like school?: A cognitive scientist answers questions about how the mind works and what it means for the classroom.* Hoboken, NJ: Wiley, 2010.

- Another comprehensive look at the science of learning, and how to apply it in the classroom.

Winter, Jeanette. *Nasreen's secret school: A true story from Afghanistan.* New York, NY: Beach Lane Books, 2006. https://www.simonandschuster.com/books/Nasreens-Secret-School/Jeanette-Winter/9781416994374.

Wong Filmore, Lily. (Various). A sample of recent publications are available at https://achievethecore.org/author/175/lily-wong-fillmore.

Woodward, John, Sybilla Beckmann, Mark Driscoll, Megan Franke, Patricia Herzig, Asha Jitendra, Kenneth R. Koedinger, and Philip Ogbuehi. *Improving mathematical problem solving in grades 4 through 8: A practice guide.* Washington, DC: US Department of Education, Institute of Education Sciences, National Center for Education Evaluation and Regional Assistance, 2012. https://ies.ed.gov/ncee/wwc/PracticeGuide/16.

World Health Organization. "Burn-out an 'occupational phenomenon': International Classification of Diseases." May 28, 2019. https://www.who.int/news/item/28-05-2019-burn-out-an-occupational-phenomenon-international-classification-of-diseases.

Wren, Sebastian. "Ten myths of reading instruction." *SEDL Letter* 14, no. 3 (December 2002). https://sedl.org/pubs/sedl-letter/v14n03/2.html.

Y

Young, Duncan. "Educators speak on mental health." Effective School Solutions, Medium, October 13, 2020. https://effectiveschoolsolutions.medium.com/educators-speak-on-mental-health-d5f06ff865da.

Z

Zeehandelaar Shaw, Dara and Amber M. Northern. *What parents want: Education preferences and trade-offs.* Washington DC: Thomas B. Fordham Institute, August 2013. https://fordhaminstitute.org/national/research/what-parents-want-education-preferences-and-trade-offs.

Zhan, Min. "Assets, parental expectations and involvement, and children's educational performance." *Children and Youth Services Review* 28, no. 8 (2006): 961–75. https://psycnet.apa.org/doi/10.1016/j.childyouth.2005.10.008.

ENDNOTES

1   Jonathan Rauch, *The constitution of knowledge: A defense of truth* (Washington DC: Brookings Institution Press, June 22, 2021), https://www.brookings.edu/book/the-constitution-of-knowledge/.

2   Zeehandelaar Shaw, Dara and Amber M. Northern, *What parents want: Education preferences and trade-offs* (Washington DC: Thomas B. Fordham Institute, August 2013), https://fordhaminstitute.org/national/research/what-parents-want-education-preferences-and-trade-offs.

3   National Center on Education and the Economy (NCEE), "Top performing countries," accessed November 22, 2021, https://ncee.org/top-performing-countries/.

4   Castles, Anne, Kathleen Rastle, and Kate Nation, "Ending the reading wars: Reading acquisition from novice to expert," *Psychological Science in the Public Interest* 19, no. 1 (June 2018): 5–51, https://doi.org/10.1177/1529100618772271; Hanford, Emily, "Hard words: Why aren't kids being taught to read?" AMP Reports, September 10, 2018, https://www.apmreports.org/episode/2018/09/10/hard-words-why-american-kids-arent-being-taught-to-read.

5   Tyner, Adam and Sarah Kabourek, *Social studies instruction and reading comprehension: Evidence from the early childhood longitudinal study*, (Washington, DC: Thomas B. Fordham Institute, 2020), https://fordhaminstitute.org/national/resources/social-studies-instruction-and-reading-comprehension.

6   Gersten, Russell et al., *Assisting students struggling with mathematics: Response to Intervention (RtI) for elementary and middle schools*, NCEE 2009-4060, (Washington, DC: US Department of Education, Institute of Education Sciences, National Center for Education Evaluation and Regional Assistance, April 2009), https://ies.ed.gov/ncee/wwc/PracticeGuide/2; Rittle-Johnson, Bethany, Jon R. Star, and Kelley Durkin, "The importance of prior knowledge when comparing examples: Influences on conceptual and procedural knowledge of equation solving," *Journal of Educational Psychology* 101, no. 4 (2009): 836–52, https://doi.org/10.1037/a0016026.

7   Jonathan Rauch, *The constitution of knowledge: A defense of truth* (Washington DC: Brookings Institution Press, June 22, 2021), https://www.brookings.edu/book/the-constitution-of-knowledge/.

8   "Practice guides," US Department of Education, Institute of Education Sciences, National Center for Education Evaluation and Regional Assistance. Accessed November 18, 2021, https://ies.ed.gov/ncee/wwc/PracticeGuides.

Ch. 1.1 – Positive school culture

9   Johns Hopkins School of Education, "School Culture 360™ for face-to-face and remote learning contexts," accessed November 16, 2021, https://edpolicy. education.jhu.edu/school-culture/; University of Chicago, "5 Essentials." UChicago Impact. Accessed November 16, 2021. https://uchicagoimpact.org/our-offerings/5essentials.

10 Shafer, Leah, "What makes a good school culture?" Harvard Graduate School of Education, July 23, 2018, https://www.gse.harvard.edu/news/uk/18/07/what-makes-good-school-culture.

11 Cranston, Jerome, "Relational trust: The glue that binds a professional learning community," *Alberta Journal of Educational Research* 57, no. 1 (Spring): 59–72, https://eric.ed.gov/?id=EJ934010.

12 Bryk, Anthony S., Valerie E. Lee, and Peter B. Holland, *Catholic schools and the common good* (Cambridge: Harvard University Press, 1995), https://www.hup. harvard.edu/catalog.php?isbn=9780674103115.

13 Seider, Scott, *Character compass: How powerful school culture can point students toward success* (Cambridge, MA: Harvard Education Press, 2012), https://www. hepg.org/hep-home/books/character-compass_169.

14 Chenoweth, Karin, *"It's being done": Academic success in unexpected schools* (Cambridge, MA: Harvard Education Press, 2007), https://eric. ed.gov/?id=ED525686.

15 Schueler, Beth and Martin West, "'It was not like a normal summer school at all': The National Summer School Initiative implementation study," EdPolicyWorks Reports Series No 9, University of Virginia, Charlottesville, VA, December 2020, https://curry.virginia.edu/sites/default/files/uploads/epw/NSSI%20 Brief_12.05.2020%20merged_0.pdf.

16 For more on Guilford County's work, see Pounds, Jessie, "Teaching the teachers: Guilford runs its own licensure program," *News and Record (NC)*, February 5, 2017, https://greensboro.com/blogs/the_chalkboard/teaching-the-teachers-guilford-runs-its-own-licensure-program/article_1d43dc0e-ebd1-5d9e-8958-8441332c8a01.html. See also Guilford County Schools, "Opportunity Culture," accessed November 18, 2021, https://www.gcsnc.com/Page/43010.

17 For more on this, see Watkins, Natasha D. and Mark S. Aber, "Exploring the relationships among race, class, gender, and middle school students' perceptions of school racial climate," *Equity and Excellence in Education* 42, no. 4 (November 2009): 395–411, https://doi.org/10.1080/10665680903260218; Adam Voight's

research summary in Voight, Adam, *The racial school-climate gap*, a report from the Region IX Equity Assistance Center at WestEd (San Francisco: WestEd) https://files.eric.ed.gov/fulltext/ED580366.pdf.

18 For more, see Sebring, Penny Bender et al., *The essential supports for school improvement* (Chicago: UChicago Consortium on School Research, September 2006), https://consortium.uchicago.edu/publications/essential-supports-school-improvement.

Chapter 1.2 – Adult mindsets

19 de Boer, Hester, Anneke C. Timmermans, and Margaretha P. C. van der Werf, "The effects of teacher expectation interventions on teachers' expectations and student achievement: Narrative review and meta-analysis," *Educational Research and Evaluation* 24, no. 3–5 (2018): 180–200, http://dx.doi.org/10.1080/13803611.2018.1550834.

20 Davis-Kean, Pamela, "The influence of parent education and family income on child achievement: The indirect role of parental expectations and the home environment," *Journal of Family Psychology* 19, no. 2 (2005): 294–304, http://dx.doi.org/10.1037/0893-3200.19.2.294.

21 Trinidad, Jose Eos, "Collective expectations protecting and preventing academic achievement," *Education and Urban Society* 51, no. 9 (December 2019): 1147–71, https://doi.org/10.1177/0013124518785444.

22 The New Teacher Project (TNTP), "The opportunity myth: What students can show us about how school is letting them down—and how to fix it," September 25, 2018, https://tntp.org/assets/documents/TNTP_The-Opportunity-Myth_Web.pdf.

23 Gershenson, Seth and Nicholas Papageorge, "The power of teacher expectations," *Education Next* 18, no. 1 (2017), https://www.educationnext.org/power-of-teacher-expectations-racial-bias-hinders-student-attainment/.

24 Quinn, David M., "Experimental evidence on teachers' racial bias in student evaluation: The role of grading scales," *Educational Evaluation and Policy Analysis* 42, no. 3 (September 2020): 375–92 https://doi.org/10.3102/0162373720932188; Travis Riddle and Stacey Sinclair, "Racial disparities in school-based disciplinary actions are associated with county-level rates of racial bias," PNAS 116, no. 17 (April 2019): 8255–60, https://doi.org/10.1073/pnas.1808307116.

25 Kennedy, Julie, "Intellectual prep: What we've learned," Charter School Growth Fund, July 13, 2019, https://stories.chartergrowthfund.org/intellectual-prep-what-weve-learned-5ce0506e03f9.

26 Achievement First, "Supporting intellectual lift in planning & execution – math," 2018, https://www.achievementfirst.org/wp-content/uploads/2018/02/Intellectual_Prep_Protocol_AF_2014.docx.

27   Organisation for Economic Cooperation and Development (OECD), "Growth mindset." In *PISA 2018 Results (Volume III): What School Life Means for Students' Lives* (Paris: OECD Publishing, 2020), https://doi.org/10.1787/bd69f805-en.

28   Lemov, Doug, *Teach like a champion 3.0* (Hoboken, NJ: Wiley and Sons, 2021), https://teachlikeachampion.com/.

Chapter 1.3 – Professional learning

29   For more, see Reeves, Douglas and Rick DuFour, "The futility of PLC lite," Phi Delta Kappan, March 1, 2016 and two books by Paul Bambrick-Santoyo of Uncommon Schools: *Driven by data 2.0: A practical guide to improve instruction and Leverage leadership 2.0: A practical guide to building exceptional schools.*

30   Kennedy, Julie, "Intellectual prep: What we've learned," Charter School Growth Fund, July 13, 2019, https://stories.chartergrowthfund.org/intellectual-prep-what-weve-learned-5ce0506e03f9.

31   Blanding, Michael, "Treating the "instructional core": Education rounds," Harvard Graduate School of Education, May 12, 2009, https://www.gse.harvard.edu/news/uk/09/05/treating-instructional-core-education-rounds.

32   Vescio, Vicki, Dorene Ross, and Alyson Adams, "A review of research on the impact of professional learning communities on teaching practice and student learning," *Teaching and Teacher Education* 24, no. 1 (January 2008): 80–91, https://doi.org/10.1016/j.tate.2007.01.004.

33   Takahashi, Akihiko and Thomas McDougal, "Collaborative lesson research: Maximizing the impact of lesson study," *ZDM Mathematics Education* 48 (2016): 513–526, https://doi.org/10.1007/s11858-015-0752-x.

34   District of Columbia Public Schools (DCPS), "LEAP: Teacher professional development," accessed November 16, 2021, https://dcps.dc.gov/page/leap-teacher-professional-development.

35   Education Resource Strategies (ERS), "Unit unpacking to methodically drive student achievement," https://www.erstrategies.org/cms/files/3504-unit-unpacking-protocol.pdf; Harvard Graduate School of Education, "Quality work protocol," accessed November 16, 2021, https://eleducation.org/resources/quality-work-protocol; Lemov, Doug, Erica Woolway, and Katie Yezzi, *Practice perfect* (Hoboken, NJ: Wiley and Sons, 2012) https://teachlikeachampion.com/books/practice-perfect/.

36   Guskey, Thomas R. and Kwang Suk Yoon, "What works in professional development?" *Phi Delta Kappan* 90, no. 7 (March 2009): 495–500, https://tguskey.com/wp-content/uploads/Professional-Learning-5-What-Works-in-Professional-Development.pdf.

37   Darling-Hammond, Linda, Maria E. Hyler, and Madelyn Gardner, *Effective teacher professional development* (Palo Alto, CA: Learning Policy Institute, June 5,

2017), https://learningpolicyinstitute.org/product/effective-teacher-professional-development-report.

38 Short, Jim and Stephanie Hirsh, *The elements: Transforming teaching through curriculum-based professional learning* (Pittsburgh, PA: Carnegie, November 2020), https://www.carnegie.org/topics/topic-articles/professional-learning-educators/elements-transforming-teaching-through-curriculum-based-professional-learning/.

39 Louisiana Department of Education, "Curriculum," accessed November 16, 2021, https://www.louisianabelieves.com/academics/curriculum; Kaufman, Julia and Rebecca Kockler, *Lessons from Louisiana's efforts to create a new marketplace for high-quality K–12 curricula and professional development* (Washington, DC: American Enterprise Institute, June 2020), https://www.aei.org/research-products/report/lessons-from-louisianas-efforts-to-create-a-new-marketplace-for-high-quality-k-12-curricula-and-professional-development/.

40 Schneider, Barbara, "Trust in schools: A core resource for school reform," *Educational Leadership*, March 1, 2003, http://www.ascd.org/publications/educational-leadership/mar03/vol60/num06/Trust-in-Schools@-A-Core-Resource-for-School-Reform.aspx.

Chapter 1.4 – Safe and supportive climate

41 *Trauma-sensitive schools training package* (Washington, DC National Center on Safe Supportive Learning Environments, American Institutes for Research, 2018), https://safesupportivelearning.ed.gov/trauma-sensitive-schools-training-package.

42 Manning, Julia and Lieny Jeon, *Teacher stress and second-hand trauma: Supporting teachers during re-entry* (Baltimore, MD: Johns Hopkins University Institute for Education Policy, August 2020), https://jscholarship.library.jhu.edu/bitstream/handle/1774.2/63228/Supporting-Teachers-During-Re-Entry.pdf?sequence=1&isAllowed=y.

43 Delpit, Lisa, *"Multiplication is for White people": Raising expectations for other people's children* (New York, NY: The New Press, 2012), http://csue402.weebly.com/uploads/8/6/2/3/8623935/warm_demanders_-_delpit.pdf; Hammond, Zaretta, *Culturally responsive teaching and the brain: Promoting authentic engagement and rigor among culturally and linguistically diverse students* (Thousand Oaks, CA: Corwin, 2014), https://us.corwin.com/en-us/nam/culturally-responsive-teaching-and-the-brain/book241754.

44 National School Climate Center, "What is school climate and why is it important?" accessed November 16, 2021, https://www.schoolclimate.org/school-climate.

45 Search Institute, "The Developmental Relationships Framework," Minneapolis, MN, 2020, https://www.search-institute.org/developmental-relationships/developmental-relationships-framework/.

46   Oliver, Regina M., Joseph H. Wehby, and Daniel J. Reschly, *Teacher classroom management practices: Effects on disruptive or aggressive student behavior*, Paper prepared for the 2011 SREE Conference, (Rockville, MD: Society for Research on Educational Effectiveness (SCREE), 2011), https://eric.ed.gov/?id=ED519160.

47   Greenberg, Julie, Hannah Putman, and Kate Walsh, *Training our future teachers: Classroom management* (Washington DC: National Council on Teacher Quality, January 2014), https://www.nctq.org/dmsView/Future_Teachers_Classroom_Management_NCTQ_Report.

48   Epstein, Michael et al., *Reducing behavior problems in the elementary school classroom: A practice guide*, NCEE #2008-012, (Washington, DC: US Department of Education, Institute of Education Sciences, National Center for Education Evaluation and Regional Assistance, September 2008), https://ies.ed.gov/ncee/wwc/PracticeGuide/4.

49   Keesor, Carolyn A, "Administrative visibility and its effect on classroom behavior," *NASSP Bulletin* 89, no. 643 (June 2005): 64–73, https://doi.org/10.1177/019263650508964306.

50   Chin, Mark J. et al., "Bias in the air: A nationwide exploration of teachers' implicit racial attitudes, aggregate bias, and student outcomes," *Educational Researcher* 49, no. 8 (November 2020): 566–78, https://doi.org/10.3102/0013189X20937240.

Chapter 1.5 – Family engagement

51   Jordan, Phyllis W., "Nudging students and families to better attendance," *Sound and Fury* (blog), FutureEd, December 22, 2018, https://www.future-ed.org/nudging-students-and-families-to-better-attendance/.

52   For more, see Sharkey, Patrick, "The acute effect of local homicides on children's cognitive performance," *PNAS* 107, no. 26 (June 2010): 11733–38, https://doi.org/10.1073/pnas.1000690107.

53   Hill, Nancy et al., "Envisioning a meaningful future and academic engagement: The role of parenting practices and school-based relationships," *Psychology in the Schools* 55, no. 6 (July 2018): 595–608, https://doi.org/10.1002/pits.22146.

54   Garcia, Maria E. et al., *Toolkit of resources for engaging families and the community as partners in education: Part 1: Building an understanding of family and community engagement*, REL 2016–148, (Washington, DC: US Department of Education, Institute of Education Sciences, National Center for Education Evaluation and Regional Assistance, Regional Educational Laboratory Pacific, September 2016), https://ies.ed.gov/ncee/edlabs/projects/project.asp?projectID=4509.

55   Dettmers, Swantje, Sittipan Yotyodying, and Kathrin Jonkmann, "Antecedents and outcomes of parental homework involvement: How do family-school partnerships affect parental homework involvement and student outcomes?" *Frontiers in Psychology* 10, no. 1048 (May 2019), https://doi.org/10.3389/fpsyg.2019.01048.

56 E. D. Hirsch, Jr., *How to educate a citizen: The power of shared knowledge to unify a nation* (New York, NY: Harper Collins, 2020), https://www.harpercollins.com/products/how-to-educate-a-citizen-e-d-hirsch?variant=33011859914786.

57 Kosanovich, Marcia, Laurie Lee, and Barbara Foorman, *A second grade teacher's guide to supporting family involvement in foundational reading skills*, REL 2021–053, (Washington, DC: US Department of Education, Institute of Education Sciences, National Center for Education Evaluation and Regional Assistance, Regional Educational Laboratory Southeast, February 2021), https://ies.ed.gov/ncee/edlabs/regions/southeast/pdf/REL_2021053.pdf; Kosanovich, Marcia, Laurie Lee, and Barbara Foorman, *A third-grade teacher's guide to supporting family involvement in foundational reading skills*, (Washington, DC: US Department of Education, Institute of Education Sciences, National Center for Education Evaluation and Regional Assistance, Regional Educational Laboratory Southeast, April 2021), https://ies.ed.gov/ncee/edlabs/projects/project.asp?projectID=5673.

58 Jerrim, John, Luis Alejandro Lopez-Agudo, and Oscar D. Marcenaro-Gutierrez, "Does it matter what children read? New evidence using longitudinal census data from Spain," *Oxford Review of Education* 46, no.5 (February 2020): 515–533, https://doi.org/10.1080/03054985.2020.1723516.

59 Sheldon, Steven B., "Improving student attendance with school, family, and community partnerships," *Journal of Educational Research* 100, no. 5 (May–June 2007): 267–75, https://eric.ed.gov/?id=EJ767721.

60 Romero, Mariajosé and Young-Sun Lee, *A national portrait of chronic absenteeism in the early grades*. (New York, NY: National Center for Children in Poverty, Columbia University, October 2007), https://doi.org/10.7916/D89C7650.

Chapter 2.1 – High-quality, knowledge-rich curriculum

61 Student Achievement Partners, *Priority instructional content in English language arts/literacy and mathematics* (New York, NY: Student Achievement Partners, June 2020), https://achievethecore.org/page/3267/priority-instructional-content-in-english-language-arts-literacy-and-mathematics.

62 National Research Council. *How people learn: Brain, mind, experience, and school: Expanded edition* (Washington, DC: The National Academies Press, 2000), https://doi.org/10.17226/9853.

63 For more, see McKeown, Margaret G., Isabel L. Beck, and Ronette G. K. Blake, "Rethinking reading comprehension instruction: A comparison of instruction for strategies and content approaches," Reading Research Quarterly 44, no. 3 (2009): 218–253); and the 2009 *Handbook of Metacognition in Education*, especially the chapter, "Writing is applied metacognition."

64 Bhatt, Rachana, Cory Koedel, and Douglas Lehmann, "Is curriculum quality uniform? Evidence from Florida," Economics of Education Review 34 (June

2013): 107–21, https://doi.org/10.1016/j.econedurev.2013.01.014; Bhatt, Rachana, and Cory Koedel, "Large-scale evaluations of curricular effectiveness: The case of elementary mathematics in Indiana," *Educational Evaluation and Policy Analysis* 34, no. 4 (2012): 391–412, http://www.jstor.org/stable/23357020; Cory Koedel and Morgan Polikoff, "Big bang for just a few bucks: The impact of math textbooks in California," *Brookings – Evidence Speaks Reports* 2, no. 5 (January 5, 2017), https://www.brookings.edu/research/big-bang-for-just-a-few-bucks-the-impact-of-math-textbooks-in-california/.

65   Steiner, David, *Curriculum research: What we know and where we need to go* (Washington, DC: Standards Work, March 2017), https://standardswork.org/wp-content/uploads/2017/03/sw-curriculum-research-report-fnl.pdf.

66   Polikoff, Morgan and Jennifer Dean, *The supplemental curriculum bazaar: Is what's online any good?* (Washington DC: Thomas B. Fordham Institute, December 2019), https://fordhaminstitute.org/national/research/supplemental-curriculum-bazaar.

67   Harvard University, Center for Education Policy Research, "Study finds that curriculum alone does not improve student outcomes," March 11, 2019, https://cepr.harvard.edu/curriculum-press-release.

68   Taylor, Joseph A. et al., "An efficacy trial of research-based curriculum materials with curriculum-based professional development," *American Educational Research Journal* 52, no. 5 (October 2015): 984–1017, https://doi.org/10.3102/0002831215585962.

Chapter 2.2 – Reading

69   Nichols-Barrer, Ira and Joshua Haimson, *Impacts of five expeditionary learning middle schools on academic achievement* (Cambridge, MA: Mathematica, July 8, 2013), https://www.mathematica.org/our-publications-and-findings/publications/impacts-of-five-expeditionary-learning-middle-schools-on-academic-achievement.

70   National Reading Panel, *Teaching children to read: An evidence-based assessment of the scientific research literature on reading and its implications for reading instruction* (Washington, DC: US Department of Health and Human Services, National Institutes of Health, National Institute of Child Health and Human Development, National Reading Panel, April 2000), https://www.nichd.nih.gov/sites/default/files/publications/pubs/nrp/Documents/report.pdf.

71   Hanford, Emily, "Hard words: Why aren't kids being taught to read?" *American Public Media Reports*, September 10, 2018, https://www.apmreports.org/episode/2018/09/10/hard-words-why-american-kids-arent-being-taught-to-read.

72   Pikulski, John J. and David J. Chard, "Fluency: Bridge between decoding and reading comprehension," The Reading Teacher 58, no. 6 (November 2011): 510–19, https://

doi.org/10.1598/RT.58.6.2; Rasinski, Timothy V., "Readers who struggle: Why many struggle and a modest proposal for improving their reading," *The Reading Teacher* 70, no. 5 (March/April 2017): 519–24, https://doi.org/10.1002/trtr.1533.

73   E. D. Hirsch, Jr., "A wealth of words: The key to increasing upward mobility is expanding vocabulary," *City Journal* (Winter 2013), https://www.city-journal.org/html/wealth-words-13523.html.

74   LaVenia, Mark. *The state of the instructional materials market: 2019 report.* Durham, NC: EdReports, April 3, 2020. https://www.edreports.org/resources/article/2019-state-of-the-market-report.

75   Polikoff, Morgan et al. *Exploring coherence in English language arts instructional systems in the Common Core era* (Santa Monica, CA: RAND Corporation, 2020), https://doi.org/10.7249/RRA279-1.

76   Pimentel, Susan, "Expanding the important national conversation about reading," Thomas B. Fordham Institute, November 8, 2011, https://fordhaminstitute.org/national/commentary/expanding-important-national-conversation-about-reading.

77   Stanovich, Keith E, "Matthew effects in reading: Some consequences of individual differences in the acquisition of literacy," *Reading Research Quarterly* 22, no. 4 (Fall 1986): 360–407, https://www.psychologytoday.com/files/u81/Stanovich__1986_.pdf.

78   *Addressing unfinished learning in foundational reading* (Nashville: Instruction Partners, n.d.), shorturl.at/bwE78.

79   Nichols-Barrer, Ira and Joshua Haimson, *Impacts of five expeditionary learning middle schools on academic achievement* (Cambridge, MA: Mathematica, July 8, 2013), https://www.mathematica.org/our-publications-and-findings/publications/impacts-of-five-expeditionary-learning-middle-schools-on-academic-achievement.

80   CenterPoint Education Solutions, "Aligning curriculum and assessments to advance achievement with CenterPoint and EL Education," February 11, 2020, https://centerpointeducation.org/news-events/_aligning_curriculum_and_assessment.

Chapter 2.3 – Writing

81   Hochman, Judith C. and Natalie Wexler, *The Writing Revolution: A guide to advancing thinking through writing in all subjects and grades* (Hoboken, NJ: Wiley and Sons, 2017) https://www.thewritingrevolution.org/.

82   Karpicke, Jeffrey D. and Janell R. Blunt, "Retrieval practice produces more learning than elaborative studying with concept mapping," *Science* 331, no. 6018 (February 2011): 772–75, https://doi.org/10.1126/science.1199327.

83   *From the editors:* For more about writing and retrieval, see "The effect of repeated writing on memory" which compares memorization among Japanese and American students using writing as a memorization strategy. Naka, Makiko and Hiroshi Naoi, "The effect of repeated writing on memory," *Memory & Cognition* 23, no. 2 (1995): 201–212, https://psycnet.apa.org/doi/10.3758/BF03197222.

84   *From the editors:* For example, in a study by Muis et al., elementary students who were solving complex math problems used more metacognitive strategies when preparing to teach those strategies compared to a control group. See Muis, Krista et al., "Learning by preparing to teach: Fostering self-regulatory processes and achievement during complex mathematics problem solving," *Journal of Educational Psychology* 107, 1–19 (August 2015), http://dx.doi.org/10.1037/edu0000071. In a study by Nestojko et al., participants who were told they would be teaching a passage had better recall than those who were told they would be tested on the passage. See Nestojko, John F., "Expecting to teach enhances learning and organization of knowledge in free recall of text passages," *Memory & Cognition*, no. 42 (2014): 1038–1048, https://doi.org/10.3758/s13421-014-0416-z.

85   DeWitt, Sharon, "The effects of note taking and mental rehearsal on memory," *Journal of Undergraduate Psychological Research* 2 (2007): 46–9, http://library.wcsu.edu/dspace/bitstream/0/65/1/dewitt.pdf.

86   Graham, Steve, Sharlene A. Kiuhara, and Meade MacKay, "The effects of writing on learning in science, social studies, and mathematics: A meta-analysis," *Review of Educational Research* 90, no. 2 (April 2020):179-226, https://eric.ed.gov/?id=EJ1249514.

87   Tindle, Richard and Mitchell G. Longstaff, "Writing, reading, and listening differentially overload working memory performance across the serial position curve," *Advances in Cognitive Psychology* 11, no. 4 (December 2015): 147–55, https://doi.org/10.5709/acp-0179-6.

88   Graham, Steve et al., *Teaching elementary school students to be effective writers: A practice guide*, NCEE 2012-4058, (Washington, DC: US Department of Education, Institute of Education Sciences, National Center for Education Evaluation and Regional Assistance, October 2018), https://ies.ed.gov/ncee/wwc/PracticeGuide/17.

89   Bangert-Drowns, Robert L., Marlene M. Hurley, and Barbara Wilkinson, "The effects of school-based writing-to-learn interventions on academic achievement: A meta-analysis," *Review of Educational Research* 74, no. 1 (March 2004): 29–58, https://doi.org/10.3102/00346543074001029; Seven, Sabriye, Asiye Pinar Koksal, and Gulsen Kocak "The effect of carrying out writing to learn activities on academic success of fifth grade students in secondary school on the subject of 'force and motion'," *Universal Journal of Educational Research* 5, no. 5 (2017): 744–49, https://doi.org/10.13189/ujer.2017.050506.

Chapter 2.4 – Mathematics

90   Fuchs, Lynn S. et al., *Assisting students struggling with mathematics: Intervention in the elementary grades*, WWC 2021006, (Washington, DC: US Department of Education, Institute of Education Sciences, National Center for Education Evaluation and Regional Assistance, 2021), https://ies.ed.gov/ncee/wwc/PracticeGuide/26#tab-summary.

91   Woodward, J., et al. *Improving mathematical problem solving in grades 4 through 8: A practice guide*, NCEE 2012-4055, (Washington, DC: National Center for Education Evaluation and Regional Assistance, Institute of Education Sciences, US Department of Education, October 2018), https://ies.ed.gov/ncee/wwc/PracticeGuide/16.

92   Schmidt, William and Curtis McKnight, *Inequality for all: The challenge of unequal opportunity in American schools*, (New York, NY: Teachers College Press, 2012), https://eric.ed.gov/?id=ED533269.

93   *Family and caregiver activity to support young math learners' understanding of fractions* (Washington, DC: US Department of Education, Institute of Education Sciences, Regional Educational Laboratory West), https://ies.ed.gov/ncee/edlabs/regions/west/Publications/Details/288.

Chapter 2.5 – Science and social studies

94   Curran, F. Chris and James Kitchin, "Early elementary science instruction: Does more time on science or science topics/skills predict science achievement in the early grades?," *AERA Open* 5, no. 3 (July-September 2019): 1–18, https://doi.org/10.1177/2332858419861081.

95   EdReports, "Amplify science," accessed November 17, 2021, https://www.edreports.org/reports/overview/amplify-science-2018.

96   Louisiana Department of Education, "Instructional materials evaluation review for alignment in science grades K – 12 (IMET)," October 9, 2019, https://www.louisianabelieves.com/docs/default-source/curricular-resources/amplify-education-inc---amplify-science-la-edition-grades-k-5-(-2019).pdf?sfvrsn=58439a1f_4.

97   Louisiana Department of Education, "Instructional materials evaluation - student standards review," June 24, 2016, https://www.louisianabelieves.com/docs/default-source/curricular-resources/core-knowledge-ckla-ela-grade-3.pdf?sfvrsn=4fe28c1f_10; EdReports, "Core Knowledge Language Arts (CKLA) (2015)," accessed November 17, 2021, https://www.edreports.org/reports/overview/core-knowledge-language-arts-ckla-2015.

98   Blank, Rolf K., "Science instructional time is declining in elementary schools: What are the implications for student achievement and closing the gap?," *Science Education* 97, no. 6 (October 2013): 830–47, https://doi.org/10.1002/sce.21078.

99   Recht, Donna R. and Lauren Leslie, "Effect of prior knowledge on good and poor readers' memory of text," *Journal of Educational Psychology* 80, no.1, (1988): 16–20, https://doi.org/10.1037/0022-0663.80.1.16.

100   Tyner, Adam and Sarah Kabourek, *Social studies instruction and reading comprehension: Evidence from the early childhood longitudinal study*, (Washington, DC: Thomas B. Fordham Institute, 2020), https://fordhaminstitute.org/national/resources/social-studies-instruction-and-reading-comprehension.

101   Willingham, Daniel T., "Ask the cognitive scientist: What is developmentally appropriate practice?" *American Educator* (Summer 2008): 34–39, https://www.aft.org/sites/default/files/periodicals/willingham_1.pdf.

Chapter 2.6 – Social and emotional learning

102   Simmons, Dena, "Why we can't afford whitewashed social-emotional learning," *ASCD* (blog), April 1, 2019, https://www.ascd.org/el/articles/why-we-cant-afford-whitewashed-social-emotional-learning.

103   Durlak, Joseph A. et al., "The impact of enhancing students' social and emotional learning: a meta-analysis of school-based universal interventions," *Child Development* 82, no. 1 (January-February 2011): 405–32, https://doi.org/10.1111/j.1467-8624.2010.01564.x.

104   Jackson, C. Kirabo et al., "School effects on socioemotional development, school-based arrests, and educational attainment," *American Economic Review: Insights* 2, no. 4 (December 2020): 491–508, https://doi.org/10.1257/aeri.20200029.

105   Gershenson, Seth, "Linking teacher quality, student attendance, and student achievement," *Education Finance and Policy* 11, no. 2 (Spring 2016): 125–149, http://dx.doi.org/10.1162/EDFP_a_00180; Kraft, Matthew A., "Teacher effects on complex cognitive skills and social-emotional competencies," *Journal of Human Resources* 54, no. 1 (2019): 1–36, https://scholar.harvard.edu/mkraft/publications/teacher-effects-complex-cognitive-skills-and-social-emotional-competencies; C. Kirabo Jackson, *What do test scores miss? The importance of teacher effects on non–test score outcomes*, NBER Working Paper 22226, (Cambridge, MA: National Bureau of Economic Research, November 2016), https://doi.org/10.3386/w22226.

106   Winter, Jeanette, *Nasreen's secret school: A true story from Afghanistan* (New York, NY: Beach Lane Books, 2006), https://www.simonandschuster.com/books/Nasreens-Secret-School/Jeanette-Winter/9781416994374.

107   Holbein, John B., "Childhood skill development and adult political participation," *American Political Science Review* 111, no. 3 (2017): 572–83, https://doi.org/10.1017/S0003055417000119.

Chapter 3.1 – Instructional strategies

108 Kosslyn, Stephen M., "The science of learning: Mechanisms and principles," in *Building the Intentional University: Minerva and the Future of Higher Education*, eds. Kosslyn, Stephen M. and Ben Nelson (Cambridge, MA: MIT Press, 2017): 209–36, https://doi.org/10.7551/mitpress/11142.003.0015.

109 Pashler, Harold, *Organizing instruction and study to improve student learning: A practice guide*, NCER 2007-2004, (Washington, DC: US Department of Education, Institute of Education Sciences, National Center for Education Research, 2007), 21, https://ies.ed.gov/ncee/wwc/PracticeGuide/1.

110 Pan, Steven C., "The interleaving effect: Mixing it up boosts learning," *Mind and Brain* (blog), Scientific American, August 4, 2015, https://www.scientificamerican.com/article/the-interleaving-effect-mixing-it-up-boosts-learning/.

111 Ferlazzo, Larry, "The what, why, and how of 'interleaving'," *Classroom Q&A, With Larry Ferlazzo* (blog), *Education Week*, May 30, 2021, https://www.edweek.org/teaching-learning/opinion-the-what-why-how-of-interleaving/2021/05.

112 Brown, Peter C., Henry L. Roediger III, and Mark A. McDaniel, *Make it stick: The science of successful learning*, (Cambridge, MA: Harvard University Press, 2014), https://www.hup.harvard.edu/catalog.php?isbn=9780674729018.

113 Rosenshine, Barak, *Principles of instruction*, Educational Practices Series–21, (Geneva, Switzerland: International Academy of Education, International Bureau of Education, 2010), http://www.ibe.unesco.org/fileadmin/user_upload/Publications/Educational_Practices/EdPractices_21.pdf.

Chapter 3.2 – Assessing student progress

114 Wiliam, Dylan, "Professional development materials," accessed November 18, 2021, https://www.dylanwiliam.org/Dylan_Wiliams_website/PD_materials.html.

115 Hamilton, Laura et al., *Using student achievement data to support instructional decision making*, NCEE 2009-4067, (Washington, DC: National Center for Education Evaluation and Regional Assistance, Institute of Education Sciences, US Department of Education, September 2009), https://ies.ed.gov/ncee/wwc/practiceguide/12.

116 Neuman, Susan, Tanya Kaefer, Ashley Pinkham, "Building background knowledge," Reading Rockets, accessed November 18, 2021, https://www.readingrockets.org/article/building-background-knowledge.

117 Nagaoka, Jenny et al., *Foundations for young adult success: A developmental framework* (CCSR concept paper, UChicago Consortium on Research, Chicago, Illinois, June 2015), https://consortium.uchicago.edu/publications/foundations-young-adult-success-developmental-framework.

Chapter 3.3 – Supports for students with disabilities

118 California State University Los Angeles Charter College of Education, "Improving instruction, accessibility, and outcomes," accessed November 18, 2021, https://ceedar.education.ufl.edu/mtss-udl-di-dev/.

119 Gersten, Russell et al., *Assisting students struggling with reading: Response to Intervention (RtI) and multi-tier intervention in the primary grades*, NCEE 2009-4045, (Washington, DC: US Department of Education, Institute of Education Sciences, National Center for Education Evaluation and Regional Assistance, February 2009), https://ies.ed.gov/ncee/wwc/PracticeGuide/3.

120 UDL Guidelines, "The UDL Guidelines," accessed November 18, 2021, https://udlguidelines.cast.org/.

121 "Practice guides," US Department of Education, Institute of Education Sciences, National Center for Education Evaluation and Regional Assistance, accessed November 18, 2021, https://ies.ed.gov/ncee/wwc/PracticeGuides; Gersten, *Struggling with reading*; Gersten, Russell et al., *Assisting students struggling with mathematics: Response to Intervention (RtI) for elementary and middle schools*, NCEE 2009-4060, (Washington, DC: US Department of Education, Institute of Education Sciences, National Center for Education Evaluation and Regional Assistance, April 2009), https://ies.ed.gov/ncee/wwc/PracticeGuide/2.

Chapter 3.4 – Supports for English learners

122 Mavrogordato, Madeline et al., "Supports for students who are English learners," Brief no. 15, EdResearch for Recovery Project, Results for America, Annenberg Institute for School Reform at Brown University, February 2021, https://annenberg.brown.edu/sites/default/files/EdResearch_for_Recovery_Brief_15.pdf.

123 *From the editors:* See the Talking Points website and WestEd's resources for English learners: https://www.wested.org/covid-19-resources/#english-learners for examples.

124 US Department of Education, Institute for Education Sciences, Regional Educational Laboratory Program, "Helping young English learners at home: Simple and fun activities to strengthen language development," February 3, 2021, https://ies.ed.gov/ncee/edlabs/regions/west/Events/Details/369; US Department of Education, Institute for Education Sciences, Regional Educational Laboratory Program, "Supporting young English learners at home," accessed November 18, 2021, https://ies.ed.gov/ncee/edlabs/regions/west/Resources/CaregiverActivities.

125 Baker, Scott et al., *Teaching academic content and literacy to English learners in elementary and middle school*, NCEE 2014-4012, (Washington, DC: US Department of Education, Institute of Education Sciences, National Center for Education Evaluation and Regional Assistance, April 2014), https://ies.ed.gov/ncee/wwc/PracticeGuide/19.

Chapter 3.5 – Supports for low-income gifted and talented students

126   National Association for Gifted Children, "Gifted education strategies," accessed January 12, 2022, https://www.nagc.org/resources-publications/gifted-education-practices.

Chapter 4.1 – Targeted help and high-dosage tutoring

127   Education Trust and MDRC, "Targeted intensive tutoring," March 17, 2021, https://edtrust.org/resource/targeted-intensive-tutoring/.

128   Steiner, David, and Daniel Weisberg, "Steiner & Weisberg: When students go back to school, too many will start the year behind. Here's how to catch them up — in real time," *The 74*, April 26, 2020, https://www.the74million.org/article/steiner-weisberg-when-students-go-back-to-school-too-many-will-start-the-year-behind-heres-how-to-catch-them-up-in-real-time/.

129   TNTP and Zearn, *Accelerate, don't remediate: New evidence from elementary math classrooms* (New York, NY: TNTP, May 2021), https://tntp.org/publications/view/teacher-training-and-classroom-practice/accelerate-dont-remediate.

130   Rollins, Suzy Pepper, *Learning in the fast lane: 8 ways to put ALL students on the road to academic success* (Alexandria, VA: ASCD, April 2014), http://www.ascd.org/Publications/Books/Overview/Learning-in-the-Fast-Lane.aspx.

131   Lake, Robin and Lynn Olson, *Learning as we go: Principles for effective assessment during the COVID-19 pandemic* (Bothell, WA: Center on Reinventing Public Education, July 2020), 5, https://crpe.org/wp-content/uploads/final_diagnostics_brief_2020.pdf.

132   Student Achievement Partners, *Priority instructional content in English language arts/literacy and mathematics* (New York, NY: Student Achievement Partners, June 2020), https://achievethecore.org/page/3267/2020-21-priority-instructional-content-in-english-language-arts-literacy-and-mathematics.

133   Tyre, Peg, "The Writing Revolution," *The Atlantic*, October 2012, https://www.theatlantic.com/magazine/archive/2012/10/the-writing-revolution/309090/.

134   Kraft, Matthew A. and Grace Falken, *A blueprint for scaling tutoring across public schools*, EdWorkingPaper 20-335, (Providence, RI: Annenberg Institute at Brown University, 2021), https://doi.org/10.26300/dkjh-s987.

135   Sawchuk, Stephen, "High-dosage tutoring is effective, but expensive. Ideas for making it work," *Education Week*, August 19, 2020, https://www.edweek.org/leadership/high-dosage-tutoring-is-effective-but-expensive-ideas-for-making-it-work/2020/08.

136   Fryer, Jr., Roland G. *The production of human capital in developed countries: Evidence from 196 randomized field experiments*, NBER Working Paper 22130, (Cambridge: National Bureau of Economic Research, March 2016), https://doi.org/10.3386/w22130.

137 Dietrichson, Jens, et al., "Academic interventions for elementary and middle school students with low socioeconomic status: A systematic review and meta-analysis," *Review of Educational Research* 87, no. 2 (April 2017): 243-282, https://doi.org/10.3102/0034654316687036.

138 Cook, Philip J. et al., *The (surprising) efficacy of academic and behavioral intervention with disadvantaged youth: Results from a randomized experiment in Chicago*, NBER Working Paper 19862, (Cambridge: National Bureau of Economic Research, January 2014), https://doi.org/10.3386/w19862.

139 Fryer, Jr., Roland G., "Injecting charter school best practices into traditional public schools: Evidence from field experiments," *The Quarterly Journal of Economics* 129, no. 3 (2014): 1355–407, https://scholar.harvard.edu/files/fryer/files/2014_injecting_charter_school_best_practices_into_traditional_public_schools.pdf.

140 Bauer, Lauren, Stephanie Lu, and Emily Moss, "Teen disengagement is on the rise," *Up Front* (blog), Brookings, October 1, 2020, https://www.brookings.edu/blog/up-front/2020/10/01/teen-disengagement-is-on-the-rise/.

141 Balfanz, Robert and Vaughan Byrnes, "Using data and the human touch: Evaluating the NYC inter-agency campaign to reduce chronic absenteeism," *Journal of Education for Students Placed at Risk (JESPAR)* 23, no. 1-2, (2018): 107–21, https://doi.org/10.1080/10824669.2018.1435283.

142 National Scientific Council on the Developing Child, *Supportive relationships and active skill-building strengthen the foundations of resilience*, Working Paper 13, (Cambridge, MA: National Scientific Council on the Developing Child, Center on the Developing Child at Harvard University, 2015), https://46y5eh11fhgw3ve3ytpwxt9r-wpengine.netdna-ssl.com/wp-content/uploads/2015/05/The-Science-of-Resilience2.pdf.

143 Carlana, Michela and Eliana La Ferrara, *Apart but connected: Online tutoring and student outcomes during the COVID-19 pandemic*, EdWorkingPaper 21-350, (Providence: Annenberg Institute at Brown University, February 2021), https://doi.org/10.26300/0azm-cf65.

144 Heinrich, Carolyn J. et al., "Improving the implementation and effectiveness of out-of-school-time tutoring," *Journal of Policy Analysis and Management* 33, no. 2 (Spring 2014): 471–94, https://doi.org/10.1002/pam.21745.

145 Education Reform Now, The Education Trust, and FutureEd, "Report: State guidance for high-impact tutoring," May 26, 2021, https://edreformnow.org/policy-briefs/report-state-guidance-for-high-impact-tutoring/.

146 National Student Support Accelerator, "High-impact tutoring," accessed November 19, 2021, https://studentsupportaccelerator.com/about/high-impact-tutoring.

147 Kraft and Falken, *A blueprint for scaling tutoring across public schools*, EdWorkingPaper 20-335, (Providence, RI: Annenberg Institute at Brown University, 2021), https://doi.org/10.26300/dkjh-s987.

148 Education Trust and MDRC, "Targeted intensive tutoring," March 17, 2021, https://edtrust.org/resource/targeted-intensive-tutoring/.

149 Gersten, Russell et al., *Assisting students struggling with reading: Response to Intervention (RtI) and multi-tier intervention in the primary grades*, NCEE 2009-4045, (Washington, DC: US Department of Education, Institute of Education Sciences, National Center for Education Evaluation and Regional Assistance, February 2009), https://ies.ed.gov/ncee/wwc/PracticeGuide/3; Russell et al., *Assisting students struggling with mathematics: Response to Intervention (RtI) for elementary and middle schools*, NCEE 2009-4060, (Washington, DC: US Department of Education, Institute of Education Sciences, National Center for Education Evaluation and Regional Assistance, April 2009), https://ies.ed.gov/ncee/wwc/PracticeGuide/2.

150 Kraft and Falken, *A blueprint for scaling tutoring across public schools*, EdWorkingPaper 20-335, (Providence, RI: Annenberg Institute at Brown University, 2021), https://doi.org/10.26300/dkjh-s987.

151 Sawchuk, Stephen, "Students lost time and learning in the pandemic. What 'acceleration' can do to help," *Education Week*, August 19, 2020, https://www.edweek.org/leadership/students-lost-time-and-learning-in-the-pandemic-what-acceleration-can-do-to-help/2020/08.

152 National Council of Teachers of Mathematics (NCTM), National Council of Supervisors of Mathematics (NCSM), *Moving forward: Mathematics learning in the era of COVID-19*, June 2020, 7, https://www.nctm.org/uploadedFiles/Research_and_Advocacy/NCTM_NCSM_Moving_Forward.pdf.

153 *From the editors:* The Mathematics Coherence Map is an online resource developed by Student Achievement Partners that can be accessed at https://achievethecore.org/coherence-map/.

154 TNTP, "COVID-19 school response toolkit," accessed on November 18, 2021, https://tntp.org/covid-19-school-response-toolkit/view/learning-acceleration-guide; Student Achievement Partners, *Priority instructional content in English language arts/literacy and mathematics* (New York, NY: Student Achievement Partners, June 2020), https://achievethecore.org/page/3267/priority-instructional-content-in-english-language-arts-literacy-and-mathematics.

155 Nickow, Andre, Philip Oreopoulos and Vincent Quan, *The impressive effects of tutoring on preK-12 learning: A systematic review and meta-analysis of the experimental evidence*, NBER Working Paper 27476, (Cambridge, MA: National Bureau of Economic Research, July 2020), 40, https://doi.org/10.3386/w27476.

156 Ibid., 32.

157 Goldstein, Michael and Bowen Paulle, *The narrow path to do it right: Lessons from vaccine making for high-dosage tutoring* (Washington DC: Thomas B. Fordham Institute, March 2021), https://fordhaminstitute.org/national/research/narrow-path-do-it-right-lessons-vaccine-making-high-dosage-tutoring.

Chapter 4.2 – Expanded mental health supports

158 Raviv, Tali, et al., "Caregiver perceptions of children's psychological well-being during the COVID-19 pandemic," *JAMA Network Open* 4, no. 4 (April 29, 2021), https://doi.org/10.1001/jamanetworkopen.2021.11103.

159 Learn Well, *Addressing K–12 students' emerging mental health needs: How educators can respond to students' anxiety and stress* (white paper, Learn Well, Plymouth, Massachusetts, December 2020), https://learnwellservices.com/wp-content/uploads/2020/12/LW_K12MentalHealth_WP_FINAL.pdf.

160 *From the editors:* See the Healthy Students, Promising Futures website.

161 *From the editors:* Those states are: California, Colorado, Connecticut, Florida, Kentucky, Louisiana, Massachusetts, Michigan, Missouri, Nevada, New Hampshire, North Carolina and South Carolina.

162 Sparks, Sarah D., "Triaging for trauma during COVID-19," *Education Week*, September 2, 2020, https://www.edweek.org/leadership/triaging-for-trauma-during-covid-19/2020/09.

163 American School Counselor Association (ASCA), National Association of School Psychologists (NASP), *School reentry considerations: Supporting student social and emotional learning and mental and behavioral health amidst COVID-19*, n. d., https://www.schoolcounselor.org/getmedia/44fe18dc-6a97-4644-950d-0799d94caaa1/School-Reentry.pdf; Romer, Natalie et al., *Best practices in universal social, emotional, and behavioral screening: An implementation guide*, version 2.0 (Madison, WI: School Mental Health Collaborative, 2020), https://smhcollaborative.org/wp-content/uploads/2019/11/universalscreening.pdf.

164 Project AWARE Ohio, "Referral pathways protocol for mental health supports," https://www.escneo.org/Downloads/Referral-Pathways-Protocol-for-Mental-Health-Supports-FINAL2.pdf.

165 Keels, Micere, et al., *Preparing schools to meet the needs of students coping with trauma and toxic stress*. Brief no. 17, EdResearch for Recovery Project, Results for America, Annenberg Institute for School Reform at Brown University, https://annenberg.brown.edu/sites/default/files/EdResearch_for_Recovery_Brief_17.pdf.

166 Substance Abuse and Mental Health Services Administration, "Trauma and violence," accessed November 18, 2021, https://www.samhsa.gov/trauma-violence.

167   Bath, Howard, "The three pillars of trauma-informed care," *Reclaiming Children and Youth* 17, no. 3 (Fall 2008): 17–21, https://eric.ed.gov/?id=EJ869920.

168   Ali, Mir M., et al. "Utilization of mental health services in educational setting by adolescents in the United States," *Journal of School Health* 89, no. 5 (March 2019): 393–401, https://doi.org/10.1111/josh.12753.

169   Markowitz, Anna J. et al., *Study of early education in Louisiana COVID-19 survey,* Report No. 2, EdPolicyWorks at University of Virginia, UCLA Graduate School of Education and Information Studies, July 2020, http://www.see-partnerships.com/uploads/1/3/2/8/132824390/seela_covid_teacher_report.pdf.

170   Young, Duncan, "Educators speak on mental health," Effective School Solutions, October 13, 2020, https://effectiveschoolsolutions.medium.com/educators-speak-on-mental-health-d5f06ff865da.

171   World Health Organization, "Burn-out an 'occupational phenomenon': International Classification of Diseases," May 28, 2019, https://www.who.int/news/item/28-05-2019-burn-out-an-occupational-phenomenon-international-classification-of-diseases.

172   Cultivating Awareness and Resilience in Education (CARE), "Research findings on care," accessed on November 18, 2021, https://createforeducation.org/care/care-research/.

173   National Child Traumatic Stress Network (NCTS), "Pause-Reset-Nourish (PRN)* to promote wellbeing: Use as needed to care for your wellness!" https://www.nctsn.org/sites/default/files/resources/fact-sheet/wellbeing-and-wellness.pdf.

Chapter 4.3 – Implementation

174   Student Achievement Partners, *Priority instructional content in English language arts/literacy and mathematics* (New York, NY: Student Achievement Partners, June 2020), https://achievethecore.org/page/3267/2020-21-priority-instructional-content-in-english-language-arts-literacy-and-mathematics.

175   Betts, Frank, "How systems thinking applies to education," *Educational Leadership* 50, no. 3 (November 1992), http://www.ascd.org/publications/educational-leadership/nov92/vol50/num03/How-Systems-Thinking-Applies-to-Education.aspx.

176   Hill, Heather C., and Anna Erickson, "Using implementation fidelity to aid in interpreting program impacts: A brief review," *Educational Researcher* 48, no. 9 (December 2019): 590–98, https://doi.org/10.3102/0013189X19891436.

177   Hill, Heather C., "Why evidence-backed programs might fall short in your school (and what to do about it)," *Education Week*, May 25, 2021, https://www.edweek.org/leadership/opinion-why-evidence-backed-programs-might-fall-short-in-your-school-and-what-to-do-about-it/2021/05.

CPSIA information can be obtained
at www.ICGtesting.com
Printed in the USA
JSHW021706020422
24480JS00006B/7

9 781915 261021